Spilling the Popcorn

The story of Suffolk's oldest cinema
and the exploits of a cinema manager

by Wayne Burns

2013

First Edition

Published and Printed by

Leiston Press Ltd
Masterlord Industrial Estate
Leiston, Suffolk
IP16 4JD

Tel: 01728 833003
www.leistonpress.com

ISBN: 978-1-907938-59-7

This book is dedicated to a number of people.

In loving memory of my dear mother Doris Rose Burns. In appreciation for her devoted love and constant encouragement. I am what I am because of you.

Neville Parry, for telling me to *"bugger off"* when I was too young to be a projectionist and for educating me in how to be a showman when I was finally allowed back in the projection room.

Those members of Leiston Town Council, who in 1976 saved Leiston Picture House for the benefit of all those who enjoy visiting the venue. There is no doubt that you were the saviour of the town's cinema and I applaud you for that action.

Bob Morris, David Gooderham and John Rayner – the three wise men!

For Christina Brown, a beautiful friend, who is so fondly remembered.

Lesley Hill, the committee and members of the Leiston Film Theatre Support Club, for your extraordinary fund raising achievements and continuing contributions. We couldn't have done it without you.

All those who have supported my aspirations to improve Leiston Film Theatre. You know who you are and you have my sincere appreciation for all that you have done and continue to do.

The loyal customers of Leiston Film Theatre – regular, occasional and visitors alike. Without you, there's little point!

And finally, my thanks go to the numerous friends and colleagues, past and present who have taken the time to share their stories and experiences with me in researching this book and to those who have offered a helping hand to make this book legal and legible! Your co-operation is so very much appreciated.

Thank you all.

Cover photographs by Tony Pick.
www.tonypickphotography.co.uk

Foreword

Well, here it is – the book I've been threatening to write for quite a few years and I can't think of a better time to put pen to paper – with Leiston Film Theatre's magnificent centenary ahead of us – and that's exactly what is it, simply magnificent.

Now don't go thinking that this is any kind of autobiography – my life hasn't been that exciting! This is simply the perfect opportunity to tell the fascinating story of one of the country's oldest surviving cinemas and in the process, share my affection for this particular cinema and my various exploits during my 25 years in the business, with an account of how, with vision, determination and the support of those around you, anything can be achieved.

So let's begin by getting a few things straight. I am not fanatical about films. In fact, despite thoroughly enjoying the experience of going to the cinema, I don't regularly do so. I probably watch more films on DVD and television than I do at the movies! People often chat to me about classic films, on the presumption that I was actually around during the days of silent movies and that I've watched every single film ever released! I normally nod my head and show an interest, but in all honesty, I haven't got a clue what most of these people are talking about!

Having said this, I firmly believe that the cinema is, without question, the very best place to watch a film – independent cinema, of course! You see, rather than claiming to be an avid follower of film, I consider myself as more of a showman and I get my kicks from putting on a show – always have, ever since I learned the craft of a being a projectionist as a teenager at Aldeburgh Cinema. Anyone can show a film, but very few can present a film and there is a big difference. I've always enjoyed the journey of selecting the film, securing the film, promoting the film and then watching the customers queuing up to watch the film.

I was born in 1970 and raised in Aldeburgh, Suffolk – in Franklin Road. My parents, Bob and Doris were hard workers – mum worked as a waitress and cleaner and dad was a milkman – yes, the milkman really was my father! I was their fourth child, with two older brothers – Rodney and Graham and an older sister Beverley. I was, as you may have already assumed a complete mistake – as I was told on occasions! There was 20 years between me and my oldest brother and I became an uncle to his eldest son at the age of 2! My youngest brother left home to marry in 1975, as did my sister in 1977, leaving me at home alone, where I was taken along each year to enjoy the variety shows on Great Yarmouth's Britannia Pier – the great days of variety, where the likes of The Krankies, Jimmy Cricket and Cannon and Ball were top of the bill and played to packed houses all season long. This provoked my love of theatre and variety – little did I realise back then that in the years ahead, I would have an association with some of these household names.

This book is not intended to be a detailed day-by-day history on Leiston Film Theatre either, although it would be ignorant not to include this, especially in its 100th anniversary. It's also important that anyone who genuinely cares for the Film Theatre realises the story behind the cinema and appreciates just how fortunate they are to have such an historic venue on their doorstep and more so, that they should never take it for granted.

In spending countless hours researching through the various original documents and chatting to numerous people who have been associated with the venue, it has become very evident that the majority of the stories that had been previously reported or spoken of over the years are something of an unintentional fabrication and that, as far as I'm concerned, this book offers an accurate account of the Film Theatre's life – apart from the 97 year old lady who told me that the cinema used to be sited further along the High Street and was moved and rebuilt in its current location, brick by brick!

We are very, very lucky to have such wonderful independent cinemas in Aldeburgh, Leiston and Woodbridge and you must support them, even if that means waiting another week or two to catch the latest blockbuster. To clone the phrase, if you don't use it, you will loose it and these places will only close once.

Finally, for those who don't know me, you'll discover that I am quite black and white in my opinions and I apologise in advance for any offence that may occur over the following pages. I'll aim to be as tactful as possible, but I intend to tell my story as an honest account and those who know me wouldn't expect anything else.

I have done my very best to ensure the details within my book are as accurate as possible, or at the very least, provide my interpretation of 100 fascinating years of history within the town of Leiston. I am very proud of my book and hope you find it interesting and entertaining.

So there you go. I really hope you enjoy the tale that I have to tell and even more so, I hope you will continue to support Suffolk's oldest cinema, during and far beyond its centenary in 2014.

Happy reading.

"The premier entertainment house in the locality"

The UK's first ever cinema that played films to the paying public was The Regent Street Cinema in Central London, which opened in 1896 and continued showing films until its closure 84 years later in 1980. There are grand plans to reopen this cinema in 2014. The first purpose built cinemas in Great Britain included the Duke of York's Cinema in Brighton in 1910, the Electric Cinema, Portobello Road in 1911 and the Phoenix, East Finchley in 1912. Wonderfully, all three cinemas are still operating, retaining many of their original features and as I'm told, thriving. Suffolk's first purpose cinema is believed to be the Gainsborough cinema in Sudbury (1912), which sadly closed its doors in 1982 and is now a nightclub.

Prior to these cinemas popping up all over the country, travelling moving picture shows would tour the land, presenting silent films on clanking projectors, powered by a steam engine, many of which were built at Leiston's famous Garrett engineering works. The films were shown in an open space such as fairgrounds and music halls where there were no regulations in place to protect the public from any potential fires. The film was made from the highly flammable cellulose nitrate base which when combined with limelight illumination, created a significant safety hazard, resulting in a number of fatal fires.

The 1909 Cinematograph Act stipulated that the projector had to be enclosed within a fire resistant enclosure and this led to purpose built cinemas opening up all over the land and each cinema had to comply with this legislation and to enforce this, each venue was regularly inspected.

By 1914, UK cinema admissions were close to 20 million and the popularity of this form of entertainment had been noted by an astute member of Leiston's community.

It was a gentleman by the name of Frank Egerton Walker, a senior staff member at Richard Garrett and Sons Ltd, who we believe noted the popularity of these mobile picture shows and had the inspirational idea to build a cinema in the industrial hub of Leiston. His desire to build *"An entertainment centre for East Suffolk"* was shared by a syndicate of local investors, including two work colleagues, Mr. James Brewster Harrison, Emerich Schmach and Commander E. B. B. Levett-Scrivener R.N. from Sibton, who raised the funds to build a picture palace in the town centre. It is also believed that as the project progressed, further investors were sought from Walkers' native Yorkshire, as well as shareholders from within the town, with an initial total of 1192 shares being purchased prior to the cinema opening, raising collateral in the region of £2,167.

At the first recorded formal meeting on Saturday 20th June 1914, a board of three directors was formed – Walker, Schmach and Levett-Scrivener acting as Chairman. Sadly, the fourth financier, Harrison, had died prior to this meeting.

Land was purchased in Aldeburgh Road for the sum of £430. The building was designed by W. H. Heath Ltd of Manchester and built by Humphreys of Knightsbridge. In total, it took less than six months to construct Leiston Picture House – the ground plan was only submitted to the building contractor on the 28th April 1914. The total cost of building Leiston Picture House was £3,057 and 8s (shillings) – in the region of £298,642 in today's money and records show that these expenses included seats at a cost of £210, a cast iron spiral staircase at £15, an all important piano for £20 and £10 for uniforms. The cinema's electricity was generated by a gas engine, driving a belt dynamo, located at the rear of the building.

On Tuesday 27th October 1914, there was a scene of great activity and anticipation, as final preparations were made ahead of the grand opening of Leiston Picture House, as it was originally known, although papers suggest that they had originally hoped to open the cinema on Friday 16th October 1914. Throughout the day, workmen laboured to complete the interior in time for the doors to open and by the early evening, all was ready, under the watchful eye of its initial operating manager, Mr. J. H. Pike – an 'apparent' showman, who appeared to come highly recommended and his original letter of application stated that he was *"27 years of age and a total abstainer."* Company minutes state that he was paid a weekly wage of 35 shillings during the construction, increasing to 45 shillings when the theatre opened.

The interior of the Picture House must have been a marvellous sight to behold and although there are no images of the completed auditorium from the day – only ones that offer a glimpse of the auditorium undergoing installation, The Aldeburgh Post commented that *"The interior arrangements of the Hall had been completed in but a few hours and one would naturally expect, under such conditions, to see some trace of hurried finishing touches. Such was not the case. Everything had a most finished appearance and elaborate too."* In the weeks following the cinema's opening, The Aldeburgh Post also reported that *"The new Theatre has rapidly become the premier entertainment house in the locality."*

The front exterior of Leiston Picture House had remained very much unchanged until 1985, when the lower half received a new look, mainly due to the safety issue of the full length glass – and in my opinion, not necessarily for the better, as I feel that greater thought should have been considered into retaining those original features. In 1914, the upper half of the front exterior was fitted with black wooden panels against a white rendered wall, with three pairs of leaded windows (as it is today – complete with the original windows, although some of the wooden panelling has been replaced over the years). There were two large gas lamps fitted to the upper half and beneath were two shops (one on either side) with patterned glass running along the top of full length glass panels on the front and a bowed full glass panel on either side of centrally located steps with a sign above that read THE PICTURE HOUSE, under which was a sheltered outer lobby, with decorative plastered mouldings on the walls and ceiling and two majestic doors, with large brass handles, which led into a bijou foyer, with further plastered mouldings on the walls and ceiling and a tiled floor. This really was a picture palace – not quite as grand as those in the major cities, but certainly a marvellous spectacle for this industrial Suffolk town.

There was a small cash desk located in the corner of the foyer, opposite another door that led to a small, narrow spiral cast iron staircase (still in use) to the upper floor. There were no other doors, except for a curtain that separated the foyer from the auditorium. As you entered the hall, a 4ft high wooden panelled partition ran along the rear of the auditorium, with the toilets located on either side.

From studying the various papers during the cinema's construction, it is generally considered that the interior may have been decorated in either dark brown, or olive green (or both), with a white ceiling, that featured elaborate stencilled patterns painted on the surrounding edges. Six glass chandeliers were suspended from the ceiling and three large circular air vents were positioned, as part of the ceiling, above the hall and also decorated with stencilled patterns – the cigarette smoke would have been drawn through these vents, through a wooden tunnel in the roof and extracted via a large electric fan and grill on the rear wall. There were also six wall air vents (three on either side) to assist in clearing the hall of smoke, odours and excess heat, created from six large cast iron radiators, which were fuelled by a boiler house at the rear of the building.

The hall was very symmetrical in appearance and the walls were fitted with identical wooden panels on each side and four pairs of exit doors (two on either side). The actual screen was simply a white washed wall at the back of the stage, with rounded edges and a decorative plastered border (the original screen and border has been restored and is still used for some live shows). There were six windows – three on either side of the hall, which would allow the daylight in during the day, with black-out blinds fitted to darken the hall for the film shows. There was a set of stairs on either side of the stage and these led to a small dressing room, with a door leading on to the stage. In the very front of the stage, an 'orchestra pit' was sited beneath the floor level – this was where the pianist would have played during the films or live programme. Although this area was always referred to as the 'orchestra pit', it was in fact, only 4ft x 9ft in size, with only enough room to accommodate an upright piano and certainly never a gathering of musicians. The 'orchestra pit' is still located beneath the stage and has recently been enlarged to accommodate several musicians.

The stage proscenium arch was constructed using wooden panels, with a plaque in the centre, on which three large crosses were painted. Nobody seems to know exactly what these three crosses symbolised. The proscenium arch was covered with material by the Town Council in 1977, which I removed in 1999 to reinstate the original proscenium feature, which was redecorated and most recently, the central plaque has been proudly fitted with the numbers 1914.

It is believed that the cinema originally had 700 seats and that these consisted of 'luxurious' seats at the rear of the auditorium, standard seating in the centre and the 'cheap' seats at the front, which weren't really seats at all – more like benches, known as the 'tuppeny crush' – so called, as they would pack them into these seats to an extent that the audience had to bunch up in order for everyone to be able to sit down. Original papers include a catalogue of cinema chairs, ranging from plush tip-up seats to those hard wooden benches.

On the cinema's opening night, an audience of invited guests took their seats for the first performance, which we are told was a Keystone film entitled *Wanted a House*, with live piano accompaniment provided by Mr. Leslie Tolhurst, who was, according to his letters to Frank Walker, quite excited at the prospect of being the resident pianist at the new Picture House, stating that *"I have sent home for my evening dress clothes and if you would care for me to wear them, especially for the opening night I shall be quite pleased to do so"*. The opening night continued with other short films including *The Battle of the Week* and *Memories that Haunt* before Madame Hills Rollet took to the stage with a performance of the French National Anthem, *La Marseillaise*. The evening had been a complete success, much to the delight of Walker and his fellow directors.

Mr. Pike resigned as the operating manager in September 1915 – only a year after his appointment. In fact, records show that he preferred to frequently move from cinema to cinema - from Castle Picture House, Durham in December 1910, to The Kemble Theatre, Hereford in May 1911, The Tower, New Brighton in June 1911, The Rink Picture Palace, Wellington in September 1911, King Theatre, Durham in March 1912 and The Victoria Theatre, Durham in November 1912. Phew!

I can't quite understand how Mr. Pike was awarded the position of operating manager of the shiny new Picture House, when his employment credentials advised that the longest period that he had worked in any one location had been nine months! Perhaps it was his glowing references, of which there were plenty – all hand written, on the same lined paper, using similar phrasing and in the same handwriting! Of course, there were no copies in those days, other than these hand written versions, but dare I suggest that Mr. Pike was not only well travelled, he may have also elaborated on his previous employment history? This is, of course, merely my own observation.

Pike was succeeded in 1915 by the 'legendary' Mr. William. S. Hammick. I use the word 'legendary' because there are many, many people who remember this particular manager for the almost regimental manner in which he ran the cinema. Mr. Hammick was a tall, thin, well dressed and groomed man, who did not tolerate unruly behaviour or noise during the films and wouldn't hesitate in throwing naughty children out of the cinema. One local resident, who is quoted in the book *The Beloved Coast* by R. M. Whitehouse, remarked that Hammick wore *"a stiff collar so high that if he moved his head sharply he would have cut his ears off"*. I've been told that during one screening, the film broke and the auditorium was filled with the sound of cheers and stamping feet, with ice cream cartons being thrown around the hall, resulting in the entire row (the cheap seats) being thrown out of the cinema. In this instance, one irate mother returned to demand her money back, protesting that her children didn't have any money to buy ice creams and consequently, Hammick refunded her money. It's also been brought to my attention that this manager had a softer side too and sometimes, when the director's backs were turned, he would allow a few children, who couldn't afford to go to the cinema, to sneak into the cheap seats during the quieter shows.

In 1916 Albert Free joined the staff at the Picture House as an apprentice, where he worked as a 'Cinematograph Operator' (projectionist). Albert quickly became more familiarly known as Toby and a short while after joining the cinema, he started courting a cashier named May. The pair eventually married and had a son named Peter. Although Toby wouldn't have realised it at the time, the Free family was going to be associated with the Picture House for the next 80 years.

The Picture House had opened against the backdrop of The Great War and the venue was the location for a number of fund raising concerts in aid of numerous causes including the Prisoners of War, the War Relief Fund and the Red Cross, amongst others, with Mr. Hammick overseeing the operation of the venue, when the cinema was filled to capacity and the company had to regularly apply to the local tribunal for Hammick to be exempt from military service, as the cinema was considered vital for boosting the morale of the public.

Less than a year after Leiston Picture House opened its doors, another cinema was opened just 18 miles away. The Woodbridge Electric Theatre received its grand opening on the 25th September 1915 and formed part of a small cinema chain operated by Ager's Cinema Circuit Ltd. With 18 miles between the two cinemas, the Picture House's trade wasn't significantly affected by the new screen in Woodbridge, which traded continuously, but faced difficult times when UK cinema attendances hit an all time low during the mid 1980's and was only saved when Pat Betts purchased the cinema in 1985, renaming it The Riverside. The cinema remains today, now under the ownership of Stuart Saunders and celebrates its own centenary in 2015.

In September 1918 a new pianist arrived at Leiston Picture House – Mr. Robinson, who replaced the initial pianist Mr. Tolhurst, whose fingers had accompanied the silent greats for four years, but Robinson's fingers were not as robust as Tolhurst's and he resigned from his post nine months later in June 1920.

There was further excitement locally – and moderate concern from the Picture House directors when, in the neighbouring town, Aldeburgh Picture House opened its doors on the 9th August 1919, to a review in the Leiston Observer that the cinema was *the most sanitary and perfect building of its kind.*" Aldeburgh's cinema wasn't purpose built – the auditorium was built on to the back of an existing 19th Century shop and the premises was sold a year after opening to Messrs Lander and Loddington, who formed a new company – Aldeburgh Cinema and Amusements Ltd. Nevertheless, the opening of a new screen only four miles away was certain to have an impact on Leiston's audience and by the early 1920's the Picture House was noticing a considerable decline in trade. In fact, the two cinemas were even in talks to 'share' performing artists, but the Artistes Federation categorically declined the notion and the Picture House was left to trade independently.

With the director's observing that, after an incredibly busy seven years trading, the hall was starting to look 'shabby', it was decided to consider spending a little money on the building and so, the front exterior of the Picture House received a fresh coat of paint and quotes were sought for new seating, but the new seats were never ordered, as by December 1921, even despite the success of Chaplin's *The Kid*, it was evident that the cinema was in serious financial trouble – just seven years after its opening and to the extent that the directors had declined their fees for the year and conceded that they would have to consult the shareholders on whether to obtain a financial advance by mortgage, or consider selling more shares to boost the capital income.

The troubled times continued into the following year and in March 1922 an extraordinary general meeting was called to discuss the financial position of the company. This was an important meeting –

even Commander Levett-Scrivener was in attendance for what is assumed was a heated debate, with the directors requesting that the shareholders give their permission for them to either raise the funds necessary to keep the cinema running or to consider selling the business as a going concern. Mr. Gibbs (one of the Directors who sold tobacco, confectionery and pastries in the cinema) proposed that they should obtain a further £500 loan to keep the cinema open, but Mr. Meadows' (also a director) counter-proposal was to sell the Picture House for no less than £5000 – less than it originally cost to build and furnish, but this proposal was unsupported by the shareholders present and a few months later, Meadows wrote to his fellow directors, advising them that he wished to sell his shares in the company – perhaps he was concerned that, as a director, he would have been accountable for any outstanding debts, should the cinema have to close.

In a final attempt to keep finances buoyant, the desperate directors approached Barclays Bank in April 1922 for a working overdraft of £1,000, offering the cinema's deeds as security, but Barclays only agreed an overdraft of £200 and a month later, the Halifax Equitable Building Society was approached for an additional loan of £500 to keep the spools turning. Things didn't look very good at all – in fact, even the Building Society recommended that they should shut the cinema, but the directors, especially Walker, were adamant that they would prefer to either lease or sell their beloved Picture House rather than see it close altogether.

By the end of the year, the financial position of the cinema had not improved and as January 1923 arrived, with the future of the Picture House looking pretty grim, the directors were unexpectedly approached to discuss an offer for the sale of the cinema as a going concern and albeit reluctantly, the directors decided that they were prepared to enter into discussions to sell the Picture House, but not for less than £4,000 – £1,000 less than they were considering 22 months earlier. However, documents indicate that, other than the initial enquiry, no further communications occurred concerning this potential sale.

The cinema struggled on regardless throughout 1924, reducing staff wages in an attempt to reduce running costs – the operator's weekly wage was cut from £2-2s-6d to £1-15s-0d. Hammick and his staff accepted their pay cuts and remained loyal to the company under the trying circumstances, while the frustrated directors continued to pursue an extension of mortgage from the Building Society and even offered the cinema itself as security on the loan. When the reply came, it was a determined decline of funds and a further suggestion that the cinema should instead be closed and while they were waiting to receive a response, two of the directors – Ted Titlow and Miss. Reeve jointly provided a loan of £1,000, on favourable terms of course, to clear the outstanding debts.

Even Hammick's position as manager was under threat and as rumours of the cinema's financial situation were circulating in February 1925, an opportunist offer was received for the purchase of the Picture House, but this was rejected by the directors as it was not sufficiently attractive to place before the shareholders. Business continued and attention was drawn to the nicotine stained hall walls and ceiling, which were in dire need of redecoration, along with the shop fronts. However, with no funds available to employ the services of Messrs Gibbs and Teager, the directors turned to the bank of Titlow and Reeve once more for a further advance of £100!

On receiving two letters in December 1926, the directors were most displeased to read a letter from Mr. R. A. Moore of Aldeburgh Picture House, enquiring on the possibility of leasing Leiston Picture House. The directors were quick to reply to Mr. Moore, bluntly advising him that *"neither his offer, nor application could be entertained by them"*. However, at the same meeting, another application was received from Mr. Woods from Bury St. Edmunds asking if the business was for sale. A kinder reply was issued that the directors were prepared to sell the Picture House, but not for less than £4,000 and consequently, this was the last they heard from Mr. Woods. Later, in 1927, Aldeburgh Cinema was leased by Mr. Raymond Rayner – a true showman – a smart man, who drove a large car and whose name was to be associated with Aldeburgh

Cinema for 38 years and later, from 1960 with Leiston Picture House.

Now in its thirteenth year of trading and having struggled through a precarious time, things suddenly appeared to be looking up for Leiston's cinema – to the extent that in December 1927, the shareholders received a 2½% dividend and the sum of £100 was paid towards reducing the mortgage – even the staff received a Christmas box and the 'sick and poor' of Leiston were presented with the proceeds of a children's pantomime of £6.00. The prosperity continued and in 1928, there was an intention to refurbish the seating in the 'cheaper parts' of the auditorium (it had suddenly stopped being referred to as a hall), to give the front fascia a fresh coat of paint and the lucky shareholders scooped a 7½% dividend. Mr. Hammick had obviously been doing his bit and was publicly congratulated on the financial success that the Picture House was once again enjoying. At the 1929 shareholders annual general meeting, a further payment of £300 was made to lessen the venue's mortgage and Toby Free's weekly wage was increased by 10 shillings, as the crowds continued to flock to the Picture House to enjoy films including *The Broadway Melody* and The Marx Brothers in *The Cocoanuts*. The good times appeared to be here once again.

As a new decade dawned and the 'Great Depression' took its hold on the United Kingdom, it was recorded that Leiston was also feeling the effects of the 'Great Slump'. Thankfully, cinema remained an affordable form of entertainment – especially the 'cheap seats' and the Picture House remained financially buoyant as a popular attraction. During 1930, the directors embraced the cinematic phenomenon of feature length talking pictures – the first being *Don Juan* in 1926, followed by *The Jazz Singer* in 1927 – the latter being the first to feature spoken dialogue. Identifying the somewhat urgent need to invest in this new equipment, which the public were *"more or less demanding"*, the directors acknowledged that *"the days and popularity of silent films were practically at an end"* and considered installing the Easterntone 'disc' apparatus,

21

but this was abandoned, in preference of the another system from the Gaumont Company Ltd at a cost of £900 for a 10 year license and a further £290 for two new projectors, with a £100 part exchange for the now redundant 16 year old equipment. The sound to the film was provided by a phonographic player, hooked up to the film projectors with large leather belts, which played wax discs and was not always successful – often, as the film played, the sound and image would become out of sync – to the amusement of the cinema staff. The discs could also easily break, scratch and were often unusable after a number of screenings.

This, of course, meant that piano accompaniment was less popular and in many cinema's, including Leiston, the pianist was replaced with other forms of 'mechanical music' for accompanying the pictures – which I presume was an organ.

The phenomenon of the 'talkies' obviously attracted the audiences to the Picture House, as did *"the careful selection of pictures by the manager"* and despite the hard economic times, business was good – with the cheap seats remaining the first to sell out – to the extent that in 1931, new linoleum flooring had to be fitted to the lower half of the auditorium and new carpets in the gangways!

Cinema was now big business and the Picture House was reaping the benefit of their investment in the new equipment, with the films *Dr. Jekyll and Mr. Hyde* and *Tarzan the Ape Man* packing the cinema night after night. By the end of 1932, the delighted directors had cleared the mortgage on the Picture House and attention was now directed to improving the venue and in September 1933, a vestibule (the lobby between the foyer and the auditorium) was constructed before *"the cold and stormy evenings commenced"*, complete with swing doors and large partition, for the grand sum of £34,15s. Three rows of top price seats were also installed at the rear of the auditorium and upholstered in red mohair velvet.

In 1934 (I haven't been able to obtain the exact opening date), yet another cinema opened locally – once again, only four miles from Leiston. Saxmundham Playhouse was a stylish Art-Deco style cinema, considered by many as a better cinema than Leiston Picture

House, with its modern interior of the time and popular 'bucket' seats along the back row. The only slight problem was the cinemas tin roof, which is affectionately recalled by those who encountered the noise whenever it rained heavily during a film. As Saxmundham opened, this affected takings at Leiston and there was a quiet rivalry to obtain the films before each other. The two cinemas were very different in appearance – the Playhouse had a tall and narrow, pillar like proscenium arch, whereas the Picture House had a mainly wooden panelled proscenium, which was shorter but much wider and this proved advantageous later on with the arrival of Cinemascope in 1953, which required a wider screen size to accommodate the projected image. Saxmundham Playhouse only survived for 28 years, closing in July 1962. Quite interestingly though, I have learned that Harry Archer was the projectionist at the Saxmundham Playhouse and Harry was my Grandad George's brother!

It is very noticeable from the Picture House minutes of the monthly director's meetings, that when business was good, they made great efforts to invest in keeping their cinema looking pristine and to keep up to date by installing the latest advances in cinema equipment. To achieve these improvements, additional shares in the business were offered for sale and owing to the popularity of the Picture House, these shares were quickly snapped up by those hopeful for a reasonable return on their investment. It is also observed that, as the various original shareholders died, their bonds were, in many situations, transferred to other family members and on occasion, offered for sale.

In April 1935, in response to the opening of the Saxmundham Playhouse, the Picture House auditorium ceiling was redecorated and no sooner had the paint dried, then a new screen, stage curtains and tracking were installed, to include a winding mechanism from the projection room – one that would be the only way of opening and closing the curtains over the following six decades. Six new Art -Deco glass chandeliers were suspended from the auditorium ceiling, along with matching side lights and to complete the look, new curtains, identical to those on the stage, were fitted to the exit doors. In 1936, the front exterior was redecorated and fitted with a large electric clock that was very similar to the replacement timepiece that is installed today. By the end of the year, the directors were reporting a substantial bank balance of £779.1s.6d.

With sound on film (that is the actual soundtrack printed on the side of the film) quickly becoming the preferred industry method, the directors agreed in July 1937 to invest £450 in new equipment, capable of delivering sound from a film print, rather than modernising the existing phonographic system. The new equipment was to be supplied by G B Equipments Ltd, who gave a confident verbal guarantee that the new apparatus would *"give satisfaction in every way"* and this appeared to be proven when the directors declared that the years trading was *"exceedingly satisfactory"*. Mr. Hammick received a pay increase of 10 shillings, Toby Free enjoyed a 5 shillings rise and the shareholders scooped a 12½% dividend. In 1938, more new seats were ordered – although the cost of each seat was astutely reduced by 7 shillings per chair, by reducing the height of the chair back by 12 inches – this saving helped the shareholders scoop a 17½% dividend at the end of the year.

In September 1939, the country went to war with Germany and judging by the director's minutes, it seems that, in response, planned celebrations to commemorate the 25th anniversary of Leiston Picture House were postponed and eventually abandoned. Prompted by fears of bombing, the government ordered all places of entertainment to close, including cinemas, but this instruction was quickly withdrawn and there is no record that the Picture House faced any such closure and continued to trade.

During the war, cinema was one of the country's prime forms of entertainment and the Picture House was packed out night after night, with customers queuing along the High Street and around into Cross Street, to catch the latest newsreels, cartoons and main feature. The programme would run for three hours and soldiers would be permitted to perch on sandbags in the aisles when all the seats had been sold. In fact, the sandbags were probably more comfortable than the cheap seats at the front of the auditorium, as it was reported that these chairs were becoming *"thoroughly worn"* during this period of renewed popularity. The directors were aware of how hard their staff were working and awarded them a war bonus of a 7½% increase to the manager and operator, 2 shillings to the cashiers and assistant operators and 1 shilling to the girl attendants and the all important chocolate boy.

With a bank balance of £1,505.1s.7d and admission prices increased to 1s.10d, 1s.6d, 1s.2d, 10d and 7d for the front seats, the Picture House entered the new decade in prosperous times and it wasn't long before 100 reconditioned seats were purchased from Kalee of London and installed to replace the tatty chairs and were fitted by Mr. Hammick and Toby Free, who were paid £6.00 for their trouble.

The groundbreaking impact of Technicolor feature films also helped to boost cinema attendances at the beginning of the 1940's with the big screen classics *The Wizard of Oz* and *Gone with the Wind* bringing huge crowds into the Picture House. Although colour films are believed to have been introduced during the early 1900's, it was the cinematic success of these two colour films in particular that introduced the phenomenon to cinema goers worldwide – *Gone with the Wind* being the first film to gross $100,000,000.

The Picture House directors ensured that regular collections were made to support the various fund raising activities to bolster the war effort, including warship week, the prisoners of war parcels fund and the war weapons week. The cinema was also asked to provide regular Sunday shows for the troops stationed nearby at the Leiston Aerodrome, which at its peak was home to in the region of 1,700 servicemen. With the influx of American servicemen in 1943, an increase in films shows was required to satisfy the demand for the military and this led to all half price admissions for children being cancelled, except for the Saturday matinees.

The show went on – even throughout the bombing raids, with one bomb exploding on the recreational grounds, showering the cinema roof with turf and debris. Peter Free once told me that, as a young boy, he was helping his father Toby to thaw out the generator at the rear of the cinema one frosty night when the air raid alarms started sounding. Suddenly there was a cry of *"Put that bloody light out"*, but with an explanation that the cinema was packed, various coats were removed and used to shield the glare of the torchlight and within a few short moments, the film continued.

War ended in May 1945 and despite the tough times of austerity in post war Leiston, the Picture House continued to be a popular attraction, with UK cinema admissions reaching an incredible 1.64 billion and the Picture House recording its highest ever admissions since its opening in 1914. With very few sources of entertainment, the Picture House was reaping the benefit of those looking for escapism in difficult times and despite war being over, the cinema continued to provide entertainment for the troops stationed locally on a Sunday evening.

In a letter dated 30th September 1945, Mr. Hammick handed his notice in to step down as manager, to retire, we believe, at the end of 1945 - 30th December to be precise and received a gift of £50.00 as a gesture of appreciation for 30 years of dedicated service. Minutes from this period clearly identify that Hammick was an extremely efficient and highly respected manager and had the sincere admiration of the directors. The vacancy was immediately advertised in a trade paper, with the directors keen to ensure that all applicants had experience in film bookings. As applications were eagerly awaited, a proposition was received from Raymond Rayner, the manager of Aldeburgh Cinema, who suggested that he could be responsible for the management control and film bookings at the Picture House – enabling him to operate both cinemas, but in a blunt reply, the directors remarked that his *"propositions had not been entertained."*

Two applicants were shortlisted for the job – Mr. Atherton of Lowestoft and Mr. G. A. Grieg of Norwich, who had been the manager of the City's first cinema – the Theatre de Luxe, opened in 1910. It was Mr. Grieg who was successful and became the Picture House's third manager on the 1st January 1946, with a wage of

£7.00 per week and one of his first responsibilities was to oversee the conversion from power generated by the venue's dynamo to mains electricity. However, Grieg was only in his position for a number of months, in comparison to Hammick's 30 years, before Mr. A. W. Chapman was appointed as the fourth manager from the 12th July 1948. There is no record of why or how Mr. Grieg left. However, he did receive a gift of £25.00 as a token of the director's appreciation and so this would suggest that this wasn't due to any dispute or grievance.

The crowds that had packed into Leiston's cinema over the years in wartime had not only taken their toll on the furnishings at the Picture House – the projection equipment was also suffering after five busy years of continuous programmes, to the extent that, in 1949 and with the sound equipment failing at times, the director's faced a major investment within the projection room.

Consideration was given to the option of purchasing a new sound system and projectors – either new or reconditioned, but Mr. Walker was adamant that the venue should ensure that any sound system was purchased as new and not second hand, although he was quite happy to consider installing a pair of reconditioned projectors, providing that these were *"in first class condition and with very little use"*. The director's received tenders from three firms and were especially keen to hear a demonstration of the RCA sound system and at the invitation of RCA Photophone Ltd, the directors Walker, Titlow and Hardy travelled to London, where they received demonstrations of various RCA sound systems in three separate locations – unanimously preferring the 'delux' sound 'reproducer' as heard at a cinema in Kentish Town.

The new equipment wasn't going to be cheap – the sound alone was going to cost £625 and when combined with two new (not reconditioned) Ross projectors, lenses and a new screen, the final bill totalled £1,370. The directors had insisted on installing the very best equipment that they could afford – little would they ever imagine that this equipment would be running up until the renewal of the projection system in 1988!

The new equipment was installed on the 19th September 1949 and despite this substantial expenditure, the shareholders scooped an impressive 20% dividend at the end of what had been a *"very satisfactory"* decade of business – one that the Picture House and the industry itself would never witness again.

Unfortunately, as the 1950's began, the meetings of the directors suddenly became less frequent and we don't quite know why. In 1950 and 1951, only five meetings were held in the boardroom above the Picture House, whereas up until this time, meetings were scheduled on a monthly basis. Therefore, it is difficult to establish exactly how trade continued at the Picture House.

It is well documented that following the post war boom, cinema admissions in the UK gradually declined throughout the 1950's but I believe that business remained fairly brisk at the Picture House. Mr. Chapman stepped down as the Picture House manager in July 1950 after only two years of service and was succeeded by Mr. J. Wilson from Huddersfield on the 21st August 1950, with a pay increase a year later to £9.0s.0d, suggesting that trade remained quite consistent and with further investment necessary, due to the introduction of Cinemascope in 1953, this new cinema experience would have helped keep the ticket office busy.

Frank Walker passed away in 1956. I would imagine that this would have been very sad day for those at the cinema – he had been so instrumental in not only instigating the construction of Leiston Picture House, but in studying the minutes of the monthly directors meetings, it is evident that he was the driving force behind the operation, only missing a handful of meetings over his 42 year reign and when he did, the meetings were brief, with no major decisions being made without him being in attendance. He had married Grace in 1929 and they never had any children. He was a well respected gentleman – an astute visionary, who brought the early phenomenon of cinema to this quiet corner of Suffolk.

The gradual rise of television, particularly during the latter part of the 1950's served a significant blow to UK cinema attendances, with millions preferring to sit in front of their wooden box, rather than see a film at the cinema. However, in rural areas, where the introduction of television would have been expensive and more gradual, their cinemas remained a popular form of entertainment and in chatting with various local people, it appears that the Picture House still enjoyed numerous packed houses throughout this period and well into the 1960's, with the *Carry On* films, James Bond, Spaghetti Westerns and the Hammer House of Horror series all putting bums on those tip-up seats and with the closure of the Saxmundham Playhouse in 1962, this would have almost certainly helped entice customers back to the Picture House.

In 1960, Mr. Wilson stepped down as the Picture House manager and it was at this point that a persistent Raymond Rayner, manager of Aldeburgh Cinema, approached the owners with a similar proposal to that of 1949, when on the retirement of Mr. Hammick, he had enquired on managing both Aldeburgh Cinema and Leiston Picture House – a notion that was, at that time, swiftly dismissed by the Picture House directors. Rayner had purchased Aldeburgh Cinema outright in 1951 and with Wilson's departure, the directors – many of which were now in their 60's, would have probably been struggling to cope with the programming and day-to-day operation of their cinema. It is therefore presumed that Rayner had reiterated his offer to manage both cinemas and on this occasion, the directors accepted his proposal and engaged him as manager of their cinema. I've been told that the cinemas would share the films – showing in Aldeburgh for three-or-so nights and then Leiston for the remainder of the week and so on, with 'showman' Rayner commuting between the cinemas on a daily basis in his large car to ensure that staff were running the shows efficiently and to a high standard.

Rayner reigned over both cinemas until 1964, when he stepped down as the Picture House manager – I believe due to ill health, as he died in 1965, at a time when Aldeburgh almost lost its cinema. It was at this point that one of the more familiar faces of the Picture House – one that had spent the past seven years hidden away in the projection room after the death of his father Toby, would take on the role of the new Picture House manager – his name was Peter

Free.

During the latter part of the 1960's and throughout the 1970's, the Picture House saw a major decline in its cinema admissions, with attendances dwindling to literally a handful of customers on occasions. A new red neon sign, with the large wording PICTURE HOUSE was fitted above the front entrance steps, but despite the now aging directors best efforts to attract an audience, it seemed that the Picture House had well and truly seen it's better days and in 1974 there was great uncertainty surrounding the future of Leiston's 60 year old cinema.

In a press cutting of June 1974, it was reported that in recent years, attendances at the now 400 seat Picture House had seriously declined, with the aging directors blaming television for the cinema's significant downturn in trade. At this time, Jack Titlow (son of the late Ted Titlow) was the chairman, Grace Walker (wife of the late, great Frank Walker) was the company secretary and Peter Free (son of the late Toby Free) was the manager and also now a shareholder. In the article, it is detailed that the future of the cinema was in the hands of Leiston Town Council and Suffolk Coastal District Council, who had both been approached by the remaining directors with an option of purchasing the cinema – comprising of the building itself, two adjoining shop units, the rear grounds and the managers house. Despite them not wanting to see Leiston's cinema close, as an uneconomic proposition, neither party felt able to commit to such a purchase at this time.

The Picture House had survived the various ups and downs throughout its 60 year history, keeping its reels turning throughout two world wars, witnessing the phenomenon of the 'talkies' and colour film, packing them in night after night when times were good and now dreading the future when things really couldn't get any worse.

Was this the final reel in Leiston Picture House's own epic story? Thankfully, the answer is no, but it was going to be another two uncertain years before the Picture House would be saved.

A cinema saved

Now I'd always been led to believe that Leiston Town Council saved the cinema in a scenario worthy of the big screen itself. Imagine the scene – a dramatic score is playing, as a man in a sharp suit, bowler hat and neatly trimmed moustache walks up the centre of Leiston High Street, carrying a contract and briefcase crammed full of money. He stops to check his watch. *"In ten minutes, this cinema will be history."* he says and lighting a long fat cigar, he continues his stride towards the crossroads. The music slows to a single violin as the camera shot cuts to the owners of Leiston Picture House, standing on the front steps, with a look of apprehension on their faces. *"This is a sad day."* says Jack Titlow. *"What's he planning to do with our Picture House?"* asks Peter Free. *"A nightclub. It's going to be a nightclub."* says Grace Walker. A solemn marching drumbeat is introduced to the musical score and the camera zooms in to reveal the man standing on the opposite side of the road looking up at the front of the building, as he begins to laugh – a real villainous roar, as the townsfolk stop and look on in sadness. The drum stops, as the man throws his lit cigar to the ground and extinguishes it with his glossy black shoe. There is silence in the street as the camera slowly pans back and then upwards to encompass the entire road. A chorus of brass is heard as suddenly, in the distance, horses hooves are heard galloping along the road and all eyes turn towards the traffic lights. The horse's legs are seen, charging past Geaters Florist and Titlows Ironmongers and then with a dramatic crescendo of brass, the horse and rider race through a red light and come to a sudden stop outside the Picture House. The music slows to a series of single piano notes, as the mysterious rider, climbs from the horse and stands face to face, staring in the eyes of the man who has come to take the Picture House – it is Bob Morris, the Town Clerk and as the music fades, he turns to face the onlookers and declares *"The Town Council are saving your cinema. Tell your neighbours, the show will go on!"* A full orchestra is heard, as the town is filled with cheers and applause and papers are seen strewn up in the air, as the villain of the piece is seen furiously fleeing the scene. Bob Morris acknowledges those in the street, shakes hands with the cinema's owners and as the credits role, he steps inside Leiston Picture House with a big grin across his face.

Okay, so I'm exaggerating more than a little, but I was always led to believe that the Town Council stepped in at the very last minute to save the Picture House from becoming a nightclub and I thought this was a terrific tale. The truth is far less glamorous I'm afraid. In 1974, the aging owners had contacted Suffolk Coastal District Council, asking if they wanted to purchase Leiston Picture House. Suffolk Coastal was not in any position to rescue the cinema, but Leiston Town Council was keen that the town shouldn't lose the 60-year-old venue.

As discussions between the Town Council and the directors continued over the following months, a house in Eastward Ho, owned by the cinema, as residence for the manager, was sold to assist in the running of the business and nine months later, now early 1975, numerous meetings were arranged to discuss options for the future of Leiston Picture House. The Town Council were keen to see the cinema remain, but were unable to commit to funding the purchase. Eight months later, the cinema was once again up for discussion by the councillors and meetings were arranged with the directors to study the operating costs, structure and fabric of the building and the Town Council even contemplated purchasing shares in the business, but that was not possible – were there any left to sell, or had they been given to Peter Free in lieu of wages?

The owners were simply too elderly to run a cinema any longer and quite frankly, they wanted rid of it and were only interested in selling the flicks – lock, stock and film reel. In April 1976, after almost two years of discussion, Leiston Picture House was finally purchased by a unanimous Leiston Town Council, under the proposal of Councillor Lenny Neale – someone who, as I have researched for this book, had grand plans for Leiston's cinema. I'm told that Lenny was adamant that Peter Free should be retained as manager until such a time that he retired or died! And that was that – the cinema was saved, Peter remained as the manager and nobody really had the first idea what to do next! Oh, and in case you are wondering, Leiston Picture House was purchased for the grand sum of £12,500.

The Town Council made a very conscious decision in 1976 to save Leiston Picture House and although it took them a while to reach that conclusion, council minutes from that time clearly indicate how nobody around the table wanted to see the cinema close. It took great conviction to take such a bold step and I applaud those responsible for their actions. There is little doubt that, without such commitment, Leiston would have almost certainly lost its cinema. So, congratulations and sincere thanks to Councillors Barker, Button, Day, Farrow, Geater, Hodgson, Howard, Knights, Neale, Neale and Telford for retaining the town's Picture House.

Right, back to the story. Buying the cinema was one thing – knowing what to do with it was another. You see, Peter had spent his life showing films, not running a cinema and it was the Town Clerk, Bob Morris, who was equally inexperienced but would ultimately become responsible for overseeing the operational side of the cinema and it wasn't long before Bob discovered that running a cinema required great expertise and many more hours than anyone had realised. At this time, the films were booked by a firm in Newmarket – 75 miles from Leiston, where, of course, they knew exactly which types of films attracted the crowds in Leiston!

The Town Council was like a litter of excited puppies with a new toy and in the immediate months following their purchase, a number of plans were formulated. The Town Clerk would start booking the films – the best films – including *Jaws*! Admission prices would increase to 50p for the seats at the back and 40p for those at the front and the Town Clerk should investigate the possibility of improving the entrance and converting the two shops into a larger foyer – an idea that would never have legs, but one that would return to haunt the council some 35 years later!

In 1976, the Picture House was in a poor state of repair and although structurally sound, the venue had remained untouched for many, many years. This was mainly due to the rapid decline in cinema attendances throughout the 1960's and 1970's and its now aging owners having a serious lack of funds to invest in what they probably considered to be something of a white elephant. Although they never wanted to see their Picture House close, I would imagine that they were quietly relieved when they finally sold the building after two long years of negotiations.

The late 1970's saw the eager Town Council embarking on a schedule of improvements. The enlargement of the stage, a new screen and sound system – which, as the records state, had to be completed in time for the arrival of the 1978 re-release of *The Sound of Music*! Repairs were made to the roof, new stage curtains were hung, the foyer was redecorated and Lyons Maid was to continue supplying the ice cream!

The improvements continued – a new exterior clock was purchased to replace the original 1936 timepiece that had stopped working years earlier and was dedicated in memory of the highly respected and long serving local doctor, Alfred Burlingham, complete with a commemorative plaque. With a gathering of dignitaries and townsfolk, the clock was unveiled by Elsie Fairweather, who I'm told was Burlingham's oldest surviving patient.

Around the same time, the cinema fascia was redecorated, the fittings in the toilets were renewed and Messrs Flick and Son were asked to act as agents for the sale of the cinema car park in Central Road – this decision was then withdrawn in January 1980.

In October 1978, talk turned to a possible change of name for the Leiston Picture House and the Town Clerk provided a comprehensive list of popular cinema names for the councillors to consider. These included:-

Moulin	Classic	New Classic
Scene	Film Centra	Royal
Plaza	Cinecentra	Pavillion
Studio	Dominion	Rialto
Ritz	Rio	Round House
Rex	Capital	Cosmo
His Majesty's	Coliseum	Celtic
Conway	Regal	Princes
Strand	Savoy	Elite
Empire	Metropole	Victoria
Prince Charles	Ionic	Palace
Electric	Galaxy	Orient
Majestic	Futurist	Century
Curzon	Palladium	Rendezvous
Royal Pavilion	Premier	Royalty
Kings	Gaiety	Forum
Priory	Grand	Regent
Embassy	Marina	Roxy
Globe	Prince of Wales	Lyric
Civic Hall	Focus	Tivoli
Astoria	Cameo	La Scala
Viking	Concorde	Comet
Arcadian		

Somehow, The Leiston Palladium, or The Savoy, Leiston doesn't quite have the same ring to it as Picture House, or as it was ultimately decided considerably later in 1983, Film Theatre.

Throughout the late 1970's the Picture House continued to show all the latest films including *Close Encounters of the Third Kind*, *Saturday Night Fever, Grease, Superman, Alien and Kramer vs. Kramer*, as well as the introduction of regular Sunday night adult films.

With the permission of the police and the local ministers, the cinema offered a weekly programme of soft porn to a loyal audience, many of which were too young to see the X certificate scenes – I've been told that several of the 15 year old 'Bog Seat

Boys' would often pack in to enjoy the confessions of a window cleaner, the antics of Emmanuelle or Debbie doing Dallas! Peter Free often told how they would all stand across the road from the cinema wearing hats and then huddle into the foyer at the risk of being seen! Later, during the construction of the Sizewell B Power Station, the venue resurrected their Sunday night smut, although this was poorly received, with one contractor storming out after just ten minutes telling Peter *"If that's the best you can do, you can stick it up your arse!"*

One or two councillors were concerned that the venue was capable of offering much more than just films and at a meeting held in September 1979, Councillor Lenny Neale voiced his concern that there was a lack of live shows appearing at the Picture House and in the coming months, the venue staged a number of live shows – mainly music hall, variety shows and band concerts. Lenny also wanted to see the auditorium walls draped, but this was considered far too costly and so, the council investigated using the services of a volunteer community service and it was a gentleman by the name of Chris Foster who approached them with a scheme to redecorate the cinemas auditorium.

Foster's vision would use voluntary labour to transform the interior of the Picture House. A £500 grant was obtained from Eastern Arts, which would cover his expenses and wages (not voluntary!) and the council would fund a further £500 and would supply all the paint, brushes, scaffolding and the like. The 12 week project would see the auditorium walls refurbished with an array of brightly painted murals of pop stars, film icons and even a map of Leiston. The council were adamant though, that they would not agree to any redecoration if it were deemed to be 'tarty', but were in unanimous approval of the proposed designs and in September 1980, paint was applied and within a few weeks, likenesses of Marilyn Monroe, Clark Gable and even The Beatles would look down on all who entered the auditorium, with larger 'theatrical' illustrations on the side walls and the vital map of Leiston painted on the rear partition – just in case patrons couldn't find their way home! Even Peter Free got in on the act and was captured in emulsion! The remainder of

36

the venue was painted in light pink, blue and peach colours – quite appropriate colours for a cinema auditorium!

Something tells me that you may have noticed a hint of sarcasm concerning the refurbishment of the auditorium. I had always personally detested those ghastly murals and considered them most unfitting for purpose. Now don't get me wrong – the murals themselves were quite good and no doubt took a lot of work, much of which as we know was voluntary. However, in 1980, with the multiplex cinema on the horizon, this type of decoration was entirely unsuitable for the new decade and I would have hoped that one of those 15 councillors would have asked if this was an appropriate image for a cinema auditorium of that time.

The newly decorated auditorium was officially opened on the 8th April 1981, with a variety show of local talent, with many of the organisations and volunteers, responsible for the new-look auditorium in attendance and to ensure that the murals looked their very best, the Picture House became a no smoking venue, much to the disapproval of numerous customers – smokers of course!

This was also the year in which Councillor Lenny Neale would push forward the notion of building new dressing rooms at the rear of the building and it was decided that, instead of refurbishing the existing toilets, new facilities should be incorporated into any plans for the new backstage extension. It was Councillor Lew Howard, a local builder, who came up with the design for the new dressing rooms and in late 1981, another local builder, Jimmy Cecil, was awarded the job of building the new facilities. Tails were wagging again and a new boiler and new stage lights were ordered to light up the newly constructed stage 'apron' – the part of the stage that extends past the proscenium arch.

By mid 1982 and funded by a bank loan, the new dressing rooms were almost complete and the old ladies toilet at the rear of the auditorium was opened up, to provide a kiosk, for the sales of sweets and ice creams (now the Showbar). It is recorded that the council met with Malcolm Jones from Knodishall, who wanted to bring live touring shows to Leiston, including music hall, pantomime and Zippo the clown. The council were enthusiastic about this idea, as this would make good use of the new backstage facilities, but shortly after, Jones intimated that he had underestimated the costs involved in bringing these shows to town and therefore, these planned shows were abandoned, much to the council's frustration. There was however, a flurry of live shows in the coming months including visits from a local touring theatre company, country and western, organ recitals, the obligatory British Legion band concerts, a performance by the Laxfield children's drama group, a steel band and a pantomime – with free apples for the children! In fact, anything and everything appeared on stage in a bid to woo an audience and one of the biggest acts to appear was The Blackdyke Mills Band, which actually made a small profit.

I think it would be safe to say that despite more people using the Picture House, councillors were starting to worry about the viability of their investment. Many notions were floated around the table on how money could be saved, with enquiries made with the Stowmarket Town Council on how they were attempting to reduce the deficit that hung over their own Regal cinema. Takings had increased since the council bought the Picture House in 1976, when ticket sales grossed a pitiful £5,716 – in fact, they had increased by £7,600 in the first year alone. Now, eight years later, this figure had increased to around £20,000, so there were definitely more people visiting. However, the operation was still running at a loss and at one meeting in March 1984, the council were noted as asking the Entertainments Officer for the District Council *"How do we persuade people to come?"* and *"How do you get through to people?"*, to which the reply was *"There is no answer to this."*

I'm sorry, but there is one easy answer to this – ask the people why they weren't using the cinema and if they had, I believe the answer would have been quite straight forward. There is a saying, which I have always adhered to – if it looks the business, you'll do the business and indeed, there are numerous local businesses that would, I believe, benefit from simply crossing the road and taking a good look at their shop frontage and window displays, but don't get me started on that subject! I believe that, despite the considerable efforts that the Town Council were making, the renamed Film Theatre had a 'flea-pit' stigma attached to it and it looked tired, shabby and needed re-branding – giving the cinema a new name was one thing, but what it really needed was a new identity and thankfully, a helping hand, to the tune of £50,000 was on its way.

Sunday 22nd September 1985 was a day that Peter Free would never forget – it was a day like any other until a serious kidnap plot was successfully executed – one that left the Town Council in shock and refusing to settle the culprit's outrageous ransom demands! The cinema was due to screen *Rambo: First Blood Part II* from the following Friday and to promote the film, a large cardboard figure of Sylvester Stallone had been placed on the front steps. With Peter's back turned (or at home feeding his cats) Rambo was stolen and a hand written note (supposedly from Rambo himself) was posted through the cinema letterbox claiming that *"I have been kidnapped by a ruthless bunch of anti-Leiston cinema thugs."* The letter continued – *"My release will materialise when ten tickets to see my film are produced."* This was a serious matter that was now in the hands of the police and in the coming days, a defiant Town Clerk, with his tongue firmly-in-cheek stated that *"The cinema would not succumb to the ransom demands"* and that *"We have issued a £10 reward for the location and return of Rambo but the ten tickets they ask for won't be forthcoming."* Rambo was never returned, although it was rumoured that he had been touring the local drinking holes before being torn, cardboard limb from limb and dumped in the streets!

1985 also brought much controversy surrounding the proposed construction of the Sizewell B power station – the UK's only commercial pressurised water reactor and the council were, quite naturally, heavily involved in the various discussions, as the potential construction would have a huge impact on the town of Leiston. However, in-between the various debates, the council continued with their programme of alterations at the Film Theatre and this included the refurbishment of the foyer and remodelling of the front entrance. Prior to this, the two integrated shops, which were leased by the East Anglian Daily Times and Lawrie Jones the barber had curved glass windows which defined the recessed entrance to the cinema – the actual original cinema foyer measured a mere 9ft x 11ft. In one dramatic incident during these works, local glazier Billy Blunden was seriously injured when his arm was sliced open by a sheet of falling glass.

A new hardwood slatted fascia was fitted to the front exterior, running along the entirety of the front of the building and over the new steps and this was stained to a dark brown colour, with plastic wording that read FILM THEATRE located above the entrance steps. The fact that this signage neglected the word LEISTON always bugged me – almost as if they couldn't afford the additional lettering, or that nobody considered that they should proudly announce to the High Street that it was Leiston's Film Theatre. That's why, when the signage was replaced in 2010 with what is there at present, the inclusion of the word Leiston was a top priority for me.

It was now 1988 and ticket prices had steadily increased to £1.60 and 80p. Sizewell B had received the green light and construction was well under way. A letter was received from the Central Electricity Generating Board, offering the Town Council the sum of £50,000 – that's right, £50,000 to spend on improvements at Leiston Film Theatre! I would imagine that, with very little consideration, the Town Council took full advantage of the grant and a grand plan of action was developed. Firstly, a new 35mm projector would be installed – with a platter system ... and a new sound system – Dolby – plus new speakers – three on stage and eight surround. With this donation came the predictable claims against the C.E.G.B. of 'community sweeteners' in light of their nuclear build, less than a mile down the road. But whatever the reason, I have little doubt that this was an offer that nobody in their right mind would reject and this meant that, at last, an improvement could be made that would matter greatly to those who supported the cinema – the experience of watching a film in Leiston.

Ordering the new projection and sound equipment was one thing, getting it into the projection room was another issue. To achieve this, the High Street was closed, so that a crane could lift the shell of the projector into the building and as an audience of onlookers watched with anticipation, the projector and sound rack was taken up the side of the building with precision and into a first floor fire escape – a very tight fit indeed. In fact, once the shell was inside, the remainder of the projector had to be built on site!

However, the projection room wasn't the only area to benefit from this cash injection. Next came the refurbishment of the 351 seat auditorium, to include new flooring and reupholstered seating – 146 to be precise, all in rich red velvet. Hang on a minute ... the auditorium had 351 seats, so why only refurbish 146 of them? This would mean that 205 tatty seats would remain. Instead, in a bid to create greater legroom, the seating capacity was reduced to 292, so there were only 146 worn seats – brilliant!

Now without wishing to sound disparaging, let's just step back for a moment and imagine the scene. We have an auditorium that is now decorated with brightly coloured murals, yellow stage curtains, red exit curtains, a mustard coloured cord carpet, a light marble effect lino and 146 new red velvet seats and 146 old ripped chairs. Why, oh why didn't somebody say something?

The remaining money was spent on foyer improvements and updating the emergency lighting and an official opening and reception to show off the new equipment and fittings was held on 7th December 1988 – just in time for the big Christmas film – Tom Hanks in *Big*.

In 1989, money had been invested, equipment had been installed and annual UK cinema attendances were recovering after a low of just 54 million admissions in 1984, but the Film Theatre was still struggling to attract an audience. The council were clearly grappling to make the place pay and were keen to consider all options to improve the situation – or possibly offload the responsibility. Much consideration was given to the future operation of the venue, including the 'American method of cinema-going' (what's that then?) and the need to make patrons feel welcome and in December 1989, it was ultimately decided that the best course of action was to lease the cinema and the now vacant barbers shop to a third party – but who would want the challenge of taking on the Film Theatre? Greg Worley, that's who.

A smouldering rumour was circulating that the Town Council had sold their cinema, which they were quick to extinguish. Then, Councillor Lenny Neale had heard that the cinema staff were being sacked and had to reapply for their jobs. Minutes advise that staff may have indeed been given notice, although I was told that a number of the 'mature' members of staff did not approve of the new boss' plans and spoke out at a staff meeting with Worley at the beginning of his lease and some of these staff subsequently parted company with their new employer shortly after. It was quite clear that Peter Free was considerably upset about the way things were progressing at the town's cinema and in all probability, this was yet another sorry situation for him personally.

In March 1990, in what would be a very uncomfortable year, Worley took over the running of the Film Theatre and his cinematic empire was born. In total, he was operating three independent sites – the Riverside Theatre in Woodbridge, the Movieland cinema in Stowmarket and the Leiston Film Theatre. The brother and sister pairing of Tim and Emma Brewster acted as management at Leiston and Peter Free, whose employment was, I believe, safeguarded by the leasing agreement, found himself back in the projection room and supervising the venue in their absence. The new bosses were young and energetic – I've been told that one of them drank champagne and had sex in the projection room, surprising Peter one morning when he walked into the projection room and discovered two naked bodies covered with a blanket! A lot of money was spent promoting the summer programme of the three venues, with films including *Teenage Mutant Ninja Turtles, Back to the Future III* and *Days of Thunder* playing throughout the entire day – morning, afternoon, early evening and night. Late night shows were introduced and I remember visiting the Film Theatre to see the film *Parenthood* one evening at 10pm, only to sit in one of the better seats, in the company of 3 others. The ambitious programming schedule must have been draining the film can dry and when staffing, utilities, advertising, film hire, rent and all manner of additional costs were taken into account, it was little surprise when the Town Clerk received a visit from a concerned resident at the end of the summer, advising him that business up the road was far from booming.

Six months on from the take-over, the lease of the Film Theatre was surrendered, due to Worley's reported 'over trading' and similarly, the Movieland, Stowmarket was dropped. It was a messy time for the Town Council and by the end of October 1990, the cinema was back in council hands – but this proved very difficult, as outstanding debts to film distributors made it almost impossible to obtain the films. The Town Clerk was dispatched to London to clarify issues with the film bosses and some staff had to wait a number of weeks before receiving their wages.

In a press cutting of August 1991, an article celebrating the 'boom' of Suffolk independent cinema was featured with the headline *'The precarious world of the independent cinema owner'* in which it was reported that Stowmarket's Movieland cinema was now in hands of a Gordon Connolly, who declared *"It's a crazy industry which has no rules."* and that Greg Worley was still in the business and employed as the cinema consultant and film buyer at The Riverside Theatre in Woodbridge.

You may have hoped that the Leiston councillors had learnt a lesson from the unsuccessful lease of the Film Theatre, but rather than learning from their experience, the powers that be decided to lease the cinema again.

In the coming weeks, as news of the cinemas circumstances spread and good old Peter Free picked up the pieces, the Town Clerk was inundated with interest from several parties – from London, Sheffield, Bristol, Port Talbot, Surrey and Leiston! Interestingly, Peter himself had shown an interest in leasing the cinema at this point, as had a certain Joan Girling, whose name will return later.

It was now December 1990 and the Town Council was approached

43

by a Mr Handley, who wanted to lease the cinema and one of the shops. Handley had claimed to have 35 years experience in the cinema business and wanted to bring the Leiston Film Theatre *"back to its former glory"*. References were sought and all indications were that 50 year old Handley was everything that he had professed to be. After the fiasco of letting the cinema to Greg Worley, councillors wanted to get this right and were impressed with new potential tenant, although Councillor Colin Ginger was concerned that if this lease fell through, there could be moves to close the cinema and chose not to vote in what was otherwise a unanimous decision. In an attempt to be as thorough as possible, a meeting was arranged between Handley and councillors to discuss his application further and in February 1991, it was decided to lease the cinema and vacant shop to Mr. Handley and that the lease would commence at the end of March.

With council cogs turning slowly, each enquiry from Mr. Handley took weeks to answer, due to there being only one council meeting each month and by the end of May, the cinema was still being operated by the Town Council and in July 1991 (seven months after his initial interest), it was reported that Handley had, without any explanation, withdrawn his offer to lease the Film Theatre.

Further interest was noted from the new management of the Movieland cinema in Stowmarket, but this was unanimously deferred, never to be raised again. It had been a bumpy 14 months for the Town Council, who still owned a cinema that some considered being a burden and with Bob Morris planning to retire, there was genuine uncertainty as to what to do next and I believe that by this point, Peter was despairing with what was happening with his beloved cinema.

The local council elections in May 1991 brought a number of new faces to the chamber table. One of these shiny new faces belonged to Joan Girling, who was responsible for staging a number of amateur dramatics shows at the Film Theatre in the late 1980's and had offered her services as a 'voluntary manageress' for the venue following Worley's departure. Joan had been responsible for the formation of the Bright Sparks amateur dramatics group, who presented their first variety show at the Film Theatre in October 1986 – a favourite tale being that the stage curtains could only be operated from the projection room and so a sign was made with the wording 'CURTAINS PLEASE PETER' on it, which would be held up to signal Peter into action, except for the occasion when Peter had gone to the toilet during the show, leaving the performers stranded behind the closed curtains - to the audience's amusement. Following the show, Bright Sparks purchased a set of walkie-talkies for the cinema, so that their sign could be binned and that Peter would always be in the right place at the right time!

With a genuine passion for the town's cinema, Joan arrived on the council scene like a determined tornado, with grand plans to ensure that the cinema was refurbished and remained open. With the prospect of the Town Clerks departure, the Town Council had to do something to ensure that somebody knew how to run their cinema – after all, Bob Morris had been doing this job for the past 15 years, and within a short space of time Joan was proposing a five year schedule of works, to update and maintain the building and that it may be prudent for the council to consider advertising for an assistant manager – *"someone with initiative"* to take the Film Theatre forward. As you would expect, it took six months from initial discussion to placing the advertisement for an assistant manager in the local press, from which 14 people applied and three applicants were shortlisted – one of them being a 22 year old projectionist from Aldeburgh. Now I wonder who that was?

" It's always a pleasure to visit Leiston Film Theatre. You are greeted with a smile, made to feel welcome and thanked when you leave. You'd never receive such personal treatment at a larger cinema.

"

Bitten by the celluloid bug

My first visit to the cinema was with my sister Bev to see *Snow White and the Seven Dwarfs*. She tells me that I was four years old and recalls that she had to swiftly remove me from the auditorium of Aldeburgh Cinema when the wicked witch appeared on screen and I proceeded to scream in fear – hardly an experience to instil a lifelong affection for the cinema business!

It's funny how music and film can help you recall a certain year. In 1982, I enjoyed movies including *E.T.*, *Rocky III* and *Tron* at Aldeburgh Cinema, although I could never see anything in *Tron* – it was just one of those over-hyped flicks, where all the kids were influenced by the Hollywood 'bullshit' and consequently wanted to see it. I would always be part of the annoying group that would occupy most of the front row and would often receive a *"shhh"* or firm warning from one of the usherettes.

So with these films in mind, I'm guessing that I was around the age of 11 or 12 when my father took me along to an open day at Aldeburgh Cinema. To the best of my memory, the tour took us around the auditorium, giving you an opportunity to stand on the stage, before moving on to that mysterious rear auditorium wall – you know the one – the area where most of us will admit to gazing up at either during a film, or more likely as we leave our seats during the credits. There was always something hypnotising about that bright dusty glow illuminating from a square panel of glass in the back wall and even more so if you were fortunate enough to catch that beam suddenly changing from one window to the other. I would often wonder what was beyond the back row and how it all worked. Well, the open day offered a rare opportunity to enter this sacred space and in small groups, we were ushered into the projection box to see the equipment in action and on entering the confines of the projection room, I was not disappointed and can honestly say that I was instantly 'bitten by the celluloid bug'.

Fascinated, I listened intently as the Chief Projectionist, Neville Parry, proudly guided the party through the various pieces of equipment, stopping to recall the odd story or two as he progressed. We were shown how to join two pieces of 35mm film together, how the film was then 'laced' through one of the two projectors and then how they would seamlessly switch from one projector to another during a film, without the audience noticing. Then, out of the blue, Neville turned to me and asked if I would like to open and close the curtains. I was shown to a panel of buttons – some would alter the black screen masking settings from 'academy' to 'wide' and to 'scope' and others would open, close and even pause the curtains, which were coloured by an array of coloured footlights at the back of the stage. I was invited to step forward and press the open button and as I did, the remainder of the group scrambled to the projection room 'portholes' to gaze at the opening curtains. Gracefully, the curtains parted and took around 10-15 seconds to reach their opening position. Next, I was asked to press the closed button and the curtains would close. That was it – I was hooked. The tour concluded with a brief cartoon show and on leaving the auditorium, we were bid farewell by an elderly lady, slightly bent forward and a little unbalanced on her legs. She was the Managing Director, Laetitia Gifford, or Lettie as she was better known.

Mrs. Gifford had been associated with Aldeburgh Cinema since 1965, when she and an influential band of townsfolk, including Benjamin Britten and Peter Pears, put forward varying amounts of money to purchase the building and become shareholders in Aldeburgh Cinema Ltd. Mrs. Gifford became the Chairman of the board in 1974, managing the cinema until her death in 1995 – just days before she was due to receive an MBE for her services to cinema. I attended her funeral, creeping in at the back to pay my respects to a lady that, as the following pages detail, nurtured my potential.

"I want to be a projectionist" I said, as Mrs. Gifford said her

goodbyes. *"Oh do you?"* she replied. *"Then why don't you come and spend an evening in the projection room?"* she continued. I don't quite recall the exact arrangements, but I do remember that a few evenings later, I arrived at Aldeburgh Cinema, to be greeted by Neville, who escorted me to the projection room and continued to tell me umpteen tales of his exploits with celluloid.

Neville had started showing films as a teenager at the Playhouse Cinema in Felixstowe and when, later in life, he worked as an ambulance driver, he still worked most evenings as a projectionist. In 1973, Neville started working at Aldeburgh Cinema, where he did so much more than just showing the films, to keep the town's cinema open. As this book goes to press, some 40 years later, he proudly claims to be the oldest projectionist working in the UK and having embraced the digital era, is still entertaining the crowds. I was fortunate enough to be invited along to Neville's 80th birthday celebrations at Aldeburgh Cinema in February 2013, where a packed house of invited and paying guests enjoyed a special 35mm screening of the 1957 Ealing comedy *The Smallest Show on Earth.* Neville always was a good friend during my later years at Aldeburgh and someone who instilled a love for the job into you, while training you in the craft of being a true showman.

Anyway, back to the story! I watched as Neville carried a heavy reel of film, which he told me would run for about an hour, before having to 'cross-over' from one projector to the other – something I was itching to see. He lifted the reel onto the top arm and then threaded the film through the various wheels, cogs and spindles of the projector, before attaching the bottom of the film to an empty reel, located beneath the projector. Neville explained that this reel would collect the film, as it passed through the projector and that it would need to be rewound after playing, so that it would be in the correct order for the following show.

I was hooked, and from the porthole, I was able to see the audience slowly filling the auditorium below. At 7.25pm, Neville lit the powerful projector bulb and at exactly 7.30pm, I watched as he dimmed the auditorium lights, started the projector and with precise timing, pressed a clever illuminated button, which flashed, whilst fading the music playing and switched over to the films soundtrack. As Neville opened the 'dowser', which allowed the light through the lens and on to the screen, he reached over and without looking, pressed the open button for the curtains and within 10 seconds and split-second timing, the adverts – Pearl and Dean of course, were on the screen.

There's something truly nostalgic about hearing that Pearl and Dean theme when you go to the cinema. It's one of those themes you instantly recognise and that infamous *Pa-pa-pa-pa-pa-pa-pa-pa-pa-pa-pa, Pa-pa-pa-pa-pa-pa-pa-paaa ... Pa* (I bet you're humming the tune) acts as an announcement to those who dilly-dally that the programme is starting and you need to get yourself settled. How many of us have sat there watching the adverts and wondered if we've got enough time to pop to the loo, or grab an ice-cream and why is it, when you make a dash for it, you return to find the lights have gone down and you struggle to remember where you were sitting? There are many people who detest the adverts and will purposely turn up some 10-15 minutes late, in the hope of walking in just as the main feature is starting. The fact is, cinemas earn money from showing these adverts and the income generated from these help keep cinema ticket prices low.

Now where was I? Oh yes. As the adverts were playing, Neville said that I could press the closed button after the last advert, which according to a hand-written sheet on the wall, was Harmony Hairspray. I watched patiently, as each advert played, clicking loudly as each join rattled through the projector 'gate'. My finger was poised over the button, waiting for those immortal lines *"Is she? Or isn't she?"* This will, of course, mean nothing to those who cannot recall the Harmony Hairspray catchphrase. Looking up at the projector spool, I could see that the adverts would be coming to an end shortly and was certain that Captain Kia-Ora was getting ever closer – they always used to play that before the main film! All of a sudden, I was filled with panic – you know that situation when you occasionally do something, like dropping a bottle of ketchup and it seems to fall to the floor in slow motion as you stumble to catch it? Well, that's exactly how it felt when I realised that I had accidently pressed the button and the curtains were now on their merry way across the screen, interrupting Telly Savalas flogging Bacardi Rum! Like a Jack Russell on steroids, Neville appeared and closed the 'dowser' and put some background music on and a little warm lighting onto the closed curtains.

An uncomfortable silence fell upon the projection room, apart that is, from the noise coming from the equipment. After a few moments, the curtains were opened, the 'dowser' was opened and the main feature started. I offered my apologies to Neville, but he was clearly annoyed and bluntly suggested that I should make my way home. I put on my coat, said my goodbyes, left the projection room and cycled home and I don't mind admitting that I cried all the way home. I felt gutted that I had pressed that button so soon and even more so that I wouldn't get to witness Neville changing from one projector to another or even rewinding the film!

In the following days, the phone rang - it was Mrs. Gifford. Mum passed the phone to me and Mrs. Gifford explained that I was simply too young to work in the projection room, but if, when I was old enough, I still wanted to be a projectionist, she would consider me again. It would be years until I was 18 and I knew that this job would be right up my street – I was stubborn and there was only one action to take – if I couldn't work at Aldeburgh Cinema, I would open my own – only this was going to be in the garden shed!

It was Christmas 1983 and while the Spectrum computer became the 'must-have' gadget, the only present on my list was a projector and I had high hopes that mum and dad would come up with the goods. The present was unwrapped and I was the proud owner of a silent super 8 projector – which was accompanied by three short films – Batman and Robin, a Tweety Pie and Sylvester cartoon and a Carry Grant western. Each film played for eight minutes and was silent – my parents couldn't afford to buy me a sound projector. I spent that Christmas showing films onto my bedroom wall but the fact they were silent obviously posed a problem, but I had a solution to overcome this – I would record my own soundtracks.

One by one, each film was shown, with me crouching over a tape recorder and impersonating the character voices (Tweety Pie was always a problem, but I was pretty good at Sylvester!) and not forgetting the sound effects. Once I had successfully completed these recordings, I would play them back – albeit usually out of sync with the actual film (just like the early days of the talkies!) I remember there was one afternoon when I had returned home from school and while watching CITV, they promoted a cartoon that was 'coming up' after the adverts. I couldn't believe it – it was the very same Tweety Pie cartoon that was in my limited collection. I ran upstairs, held my tape recorder against the television speaker and recorded the actual soundtrack – how lucky was that?

In 1983, I continued to enjoy the latest films up on Aldeburgh's silver screen, including my first 3D encounter with *Jaws 3D*. It was a big deal when 3D came to Aldeburgh, with long queues stretching along the High Street and I can still remember wearing my cardboard red and green 3D glasses, complete with *Jaws 3D* logo on the front and trying to grab hold of a severed arm that was floating across the auditorium towards me – only to be the recipient of a 'tut' from a lady in front, who suddenly had my hand patting her head! It was in this cinematic year, that one certain film would see me transform the shed at home into Franklin Cinema!

The film in question was Octopussy, with Roger Moore returning as James Bond 007. For some reason it was one of those films that I went to see many times while it was showing in Aldeburgh and I stayed glued to my seat on every occasion. In fact, I was so fascinated by the film, I saved up and ordered the soundtrack - on cassette of course, from the Aldeburgh Music Shop. This took weeks to arrive and when it did, I almost wore it out after rewinding it to replay *All Time High* by Rita Coolidge!

We had a brick shed at home in Franklin Road, which over the years had been used as a puppet theatre, a miniature fun-fair and now it was time for the family shed to become a cinema! First a coat of grey paint was applied to the walls to darken the interior. An old window blind, which was patterned on one side but conveniently white on the other, was hung beneath a shelf to act as a screen. A curtain track was fixed beneath the shelf and a pair curtains were hung, with a length of string attached to each leading curtain runner and then threaded though numerous hooks to the back of the shed. Three long boards were laid on top of bricks – the back row was four bricks high, the centre had three bricks and so on and a layer of padded lagging was placed on top of each board. A sheet of wood, with a square hole cut out in the centre was balanced behind the rows of seats, in front of a tumble dryer, on which the 'silent' super 8 projector was installed, along with my trusty tape recorder alongside, to provide the music and soundtracks!

Leaflets promoting the programme of Franklin Cinema were created, using those handy sheets of transfer lettering – the kind that had lots of fonts to choose from and where, if you weren't careful and didn't rub the whole letter, you would remove the sheet and find that you only had half a letter on the paper. These programmes were photo-copied and handed out to local children, who would pack into the shed most weekends to watch the limited selection of super-heroes, cartoon characters, or cowboys and Indians!

I can even remember once bumping into Mrs. Gifford when I was photo-copying my leaflets at the library and proudly telling her that I had my own cinema in the shed, which she found quite amusing, along with the fact that I was buying choc-ices from Bellings shop and selling these during the intermission!

While I was writing this book, I asked my father what he and my mother honestly thought about my commandeering the shed and inviting hoards of children to watch films. After a little thought, he simply commented that it was a nuisance – the fact that their belongings were removed from the shed and that they could never get to the tumble dryer was an inconvenience, but he did confirm that it was mum who would always say *"he's happy, leave him alone."*

In the coming years, I took up other interests, like Punch and Judy and playing the drums in the Leiston High School Wind Band and somehow, Mrs. Gifford and I would cross paths on many occasions and I always found her to be engaging and encouraging.

I left school in 1986 and enrolled on a Theatre and Leisure Studies course at Lowestoft College, which was split equally between the college itself and the Seagull Theatre. I have to confess, I would often bunk-off certain subjects, in favour of sitting on the beach watching the Punch and Judy show, but would never miss any of the practical studies at the theatre and thoroughly enjoyed my time on this course, meeting some bizarre characters along the way and well and truly opening my eyes to life outside Aldeburgh!

After I left college in 1987, I immediately started work for Tanners Dairy, which quickly became Dairy Crest. Passing my driving test, I was given my own milk round, which although the earnings were excellent for a lad of 17 years, it was far from my ideal vocation.

When I finally turned 18, the family threw a small surprise gathering for me. Mum had been ill, after suffering with severe asthma for several years and had been in and out of hospital on several occasions and although she was obviously unwell on that evening, she was determined that I should celebrate my 18th birthday. I felt stuck in a complete rut – I didn't want to spend my life doing doorstep deliveries and needed something to do – something that actually interested me.

I can't remember if I called her, or simply went and knocked on her door, but I contacted Mrs. Gifford and gently reminded her of a conversation we had several years earlier. Whether she actually remembered that conversation is another thing, but she did once again invite me to spend an evening in the projection room *"to see what Neville thought!"* As I knocked on the projection room door a few nights later, the door opened and there stood a slightly older looking Neville who greeted me with the words *"Not you again!"*

I was very lucky that Neville had 15 years experience in the projection room at Aldeburgh Cinema – 35 years if you include his time elsewhere. It seemed that there wasn't anything he didn't know about the job and he was keen to share that knowledge with you – usually through the odd tale or two, taking time to fully explain the why, when and how. He was (and still is) a true showman and took great pride in putting on a good show – the lights had to be dimmed

54

in a particular manner, the curtains had to be opened at a certain time and the film had to be treated with the utmost respect. The fact is, as Neville pointed out, not just anyone can be a projectionist – you either had 'it' or you didn't. I spent many, many weeks watching Neville at work – preparing the film, cleaning the projectors and running the show. He would stand beside me, explaining things in great detail when I was learning the craft and then politely correcting my mistakes when I'd done something wrong. It was evident that he was never going to let me run a show alone until he was absolutely certain that I was entirely competent and when that time finally came, I think we both knew I had 'it'!

1989 was a year that changed my life. It was the year that my dear mother died, aged 59. I was 18 years old and suddenly, I was without a mum. Her asthma had progressed to emphysema, brought on by years of heavy smoking, which eventually turned to lung cancer and that was it. She came out of hospital having been given a week to live and she died exactly seven days later. It was an awful time – it all happened so quickly. I suffered from depression for a number of months as a result and felt totally isolated. My brothers and sister had their families for support but I was living at home at the time and my relationship with my father was far from harmonious – in fact we hardly got along at all and the hurt and anger that we were both feeling after losing a wife and mother didn't help either. It was a shitty situation. I was working on the milk round, but as I've already stated, I hated the bloody job, so I threw myself into my entertaining and cinema work and it was the latter that provided the distraction through a truly sad period.

My mother had always supported me in all that I did and where at times some of my madcap schemes must have surely driven my parents crazy, she always encouraged me. When I reflect on that particular moment in my life, I honestly believe that I developed a determination to make her proud of me and to prove that all those who had sniggered at my childhood antics would be, as my mother had always maintained, proven wrong. My mother's sudden death was the one event that completely altered my outlook on life, probably for the better.

I would work on the milk round from midnight until 9am, then home for a sleep, followed by an afternoon on Aldeburgh beach with my Punch and Judy show and an evening in the projection room, followed by a pint at The Cross Keys – and so it went on. There were numerous nights when I would sit in the comfort of the warm projection room, yawning and gazing up at the film spool, knowing that I would have to 'change-over' from one projector to the other in around 10 minutes, I would just rest my tired eyes for a few minutes, only to be woken by the telephone ringing – it was the box office staff, phoning through to let me know that the screen had turned bright white! That's right, I'd fallen asleep and missed the change-over – that chair was just too darn comfy!

There was another night when Mrs Gifford had scheduled a late night screening of *Sleeping With The Enemy*, which was playing over the top of *The Naked Gun 33 1/3: The Smell of Fear*. At the end of reel three, I changed over to the next spool and realised that I was showing reel four of the wrong film. One minute the audience were watching Julia Roberts in the bath and in a split second, Leslie Neilson was grabbing hold of a woman's breast! Within a couple of minutes, Julia Roberts was back on screen, climbing out of the bath. And the best bit – nobody even left their seats to let the box office know!

I was very popular with my Dairy Crest customers – I would set out shortly after midnight to make sure they got their milk in time for breakfast, not lunch! There was another reason for me being up and about so early in the morning – I was delivering on the busy A12 and I wanted to be clear of this stretch of road before alarm clocks started ringing and the busy morning commute began. I also had the responsibility of delivering hundreds of pints daily to the canteen on the Sizewell B site and as part of this contract, I had to get the milk delivered by a certain time. The traffic would be queued up all the way from the site to the Leiston turn off, with little chance of overtaking, so I would boycott this traffic jam by driving the milk float in the opposite lane, sharing the pavement and the road!

The Sizewell B canteen unknowingly helped me to become the

leading Dairy Crest salesman in East Anglia. There was a national campaign to get more customers taking up a healthier lifestyle by changing from full fat silver top to blue top skimmed milk. Dairy Crest launched a promotion and the milkman who was responsible for the biggest increase in skimmed milk sales would win a cash prize and a pocket TV. I wanted to win and I conjured up a scheme to help me secure the prize – I would change the Sizewell B canteen over to skimmed milk! The dairy had a clever gizmo, which would allow you to re-top the bottles, where the foil tops had split. My plan was easy – I would remove all the blue skimmed bottle tops and replace them with silver full fat tops and nobody should be the wiser – and they weren't. In fact, the canteen was getting through so much milk, because the skimmed milk was far thinner than the creamy version, that they increased their order – fantastic! I won the cash and the TV and was responsible for the healthier diet for thousands of contractors in the process!

I was very friendly with an American couple, Karen and Chris Huebner – he worked for the USAF at Bentwaters and she was the secretary at Dairy Crest. They were both great friends and I would spend many hours in their company, both out on the Base and at their home. In the April of 1990, Chris, Karen, her brother and sister -in-law invited me to travel to Edinburgh with them, where we did all the tourist stuff and got drunk – very drunk. It was while I was in Scotland that I decided to do something about my weight. I'd always been fat – ever since I fell victim to the tuck shop in the middle school and had ballooned to 17 stone during my late teens. I had tried to lose weight several times over the years but for some reason, I was now completely focused on succeeding and on returning to Suffolk, I continued to cut out the bad stuff and take more exercise – it wasn't that hard really once a routine was formed. I would run up and down the paths while out delivering milk, I would aim to cycle 10 miles, five times a week and I stopped buying bacon rolls and chocolate – and the weight fell off. I needed a goal and perhaps to escape for a bit and so arranged to go and stay with my aunt Jenny (mum's sister) and uncle Jimmy in Florida and six months later, as I left for the airport, I had lost exactly seven stone in weight – and for the first time in a long while, I felt bloody fantastic. But something happened 24 hours before I flew out of the UK, which would once again make an indentation on my future career path.

The day before I was due to leave for Florida, I returned to the milk depot and was asked to go to the office. Once inside, the manager, Derek, handed me a letter and explained that he was concerned that my outside interests were conflicting with my duties at Dairy Crest. It was suggested that my entertaining and cinema work were taking preference over my doorstep deliveries and that this caused Derek great concern. What followed was a brief discussion, where I strongly disagreed and argued that all my customers and the all-important Sizewell B site received their deliveries before 9am, whereas other milkmen were still out delivering well after midday. I continued with a statement that what I did when I was away from the dairy was entirely my business. There was a stand off – Derek was firm on his decision and had really annoyed me. I loved my cinema work and hated the milk round. I was seven stone lighter and off to Florida in 24 hours and couldn't really give a damn and so right there and then, I made a decision. As I remember it, I stood up, removed my money bag from around my neck, handed it to Derek and told him to stuff his bloody job up his arse and walked out. I cycled home, calling Derek every name imaginable under my breath and 24 hours later, I flew out of the UK knowing that I would return without a full time job, but when I did finally return, my future was about to well and truly take shape.

I was determined not to worry about my employment issue while I was away – I was on holiday after all and I'd worked jolly hard for it. On returning to Aldeburgh however, I couldn't help but wonder what I was going to do. I arrived home and the phone rang – it was Mrs. Gifford, asking if I would pay her a visit. I went straight away, not quite sure what she wanted me for. It transpired that she had learnt of my departure from full time employment while I was away and she had a proposal for me. I was offered a position as projectionist, caretaker and anything else they wanted to do with me! I gratefully accepted and would become responsible for the cleaning and general maintenance of the cinema along with the day-to-day projectionist duties. I was quite happy – I wasn't earning as much money, but I was content. The only problem was a certain enemy named Harry.

Mrs. Gifford had a scruffy Jack Russell named Harry, or as I called it, a snappy little b*****d! Harry's coat resembled one of those long fur rugs that had never been washed and the dog would be let in to wonder through the auditorium most mornings to eat the food debris that was left on the auditorium floor. Harry would then spend the remainder of his morning sitting at the top of the stairs, outside the cinema office, looking sweet and innocent. In the event that I had to go upstairs, the dog would sit and watch me climb the stairs, looking up at me with sad looking puppy dog eyes – you know the type, where you feel compelled to give the dog a pat. The dog never received a fuss from me for one very good reason – Harry would watch me climb the stairs and walk past him. On my return, Harry would once again gaze up at me and then, as I tread the top step, the dog would snarl and try to bite me and on several occasions, he did. I swear that, as time went on, I could almost hear Harry snigger to himself once I had reached the bottom step!

And so there I was. I would polish the foyer floor, sweep and vacuum the auditorium, mop the toilets and then attend to anything else that required attention. I worked at my own pace and made sure that everywhere, especially the projection room, was kept in good nick. I would have the afternoon off – or on the beach, entertaining the crowds with my Punch and Judy show and then back to the cinema to show the films in the evening. It was a good time.

1991 saw the arrival of newbie projectionist Nick Ash at Aldeburgh Cinema. Nick was a lanky lad, who was as disorganised as they came, but had a genuine enjoyment in showing films and we got along very well. We shared many laughs and drinks at the Cross Keys and between us were responsible for a fund raising event to boost cinema funds and see the sights in the process. The aim of the challenge was to visit as many UK cinemas as we could in one week – an ambitious task, which became known as 'The Great

Cinema Chase'. Sponsorship forms were completed and with the backing of the Prime Minister and Prince Charles, we set off, with our journey taking us across Suffolk, down to London, on to the Midlands, down south, across to the Isle of Wight, up to Yorkshire and returning via Norfolk.

We slept in the back of the car and when we missed the last ferry from the Isle of Wight, we spent the night under a bridge! The car broke down; we out-ran muggers in Oxford and made daily live phone-ins to BBC Radio Suffolk, who followed our adventure 'on air' throughout the week. 171 cinemas were visited in total and over £1,000 was raised in the process.

It was during this fund raising effort that I encountered the Chief Projectionist at The Empire, Leicester Square, who had looked after us so well when we paid them a visit during that cinema chase. Ilka took us on a grand tour of the iconic West End venue – a real eye opener for us two Suffolk boys and this included time spent in the projection room. I was in my element and we were invited to keep in touch – which we did, travelling to London on numerous occasions to sneak in to several advance screenings, weeks before their UK release and on one occasion, the staff of the Empire travelled up to visit us in Aldeburgh.

I can't recall a time when Mrs. Gifford and I really had a cross word. If she was unhappy about something, she would tell you and you would deal with it. I didn't really give her any cause to doubt my ability. She didn't understand the workings of the projection room and therefore, rarely interfered in this area. In fact, that's exactly how the cinema ran – projectionists didn't interfere in the duties of the front-of-house staff and vice-versa and this ethic was proven to work well and I eventually took this approach to Leiston Film Theatre.

At Aldeburgh, once the main film had started, the box office staff would ring through and let you know that a coffee was ready. One night, Neville and I were in the box, when the phone rang – there was a problem. Front-of-house had run out of milk. Neville was most upset and wasn't about to drink a black coffee. Threatening to turn the projector off, if he didn't get his cup of coffee, Neville suggested that the box office staff might like to use a tub of ice cream – which they did. I don't believe that Neville would have actually switched the equipment off – he just enjoyed winding the front-of-house staff up – like the time he had one of his grandchildren's toys in his pocket that made a beeping noise – he told the box office staff that it was coming from the telephone and that they had been featured on television as being extremely dangerous! That's the sort of nonsense that we would concoct to amuse ourselves when we weren't busy.

In early 1992, Aldeburgh underwent the installation of the very latest in Dolby digital surround sound and it was amazing. I never thought the previous sound system was good at Aldeburgh, but kept my mouth shut, as Neville had something to do with the system that was installed. The equipment arrived, followed by the technician. Steve Grant was a larger than life character from Canvey Island who was very knowledgeable when it came to all things Dolby. Next, Jason and Matt – the electricians from Bayfield's were on site, to wire the new speakers in behind the screen and on the auditorium walls. It was going to take five days to install and during that time, everyone got on very well and I was on site to help as necessary. Day four came – 1st April and the electrical team and I hatched a plan make Steve an April Fool. The proposal was that at exactly 11am, Jason would lay a ladder on the floor and pretend to have fallen off – we would let Steve think that Jason had injured himself. A horrible scheme I know, but Steve had spent the entire week winding us all up and now it was our turn. It was approaching 11 o'clock, Steve was in the projection room wiring up the sound rack, Matt was up in the roof and I was behind the screen. All of a sudden, there was a crash, a moan and then a cry of help. Steve abandoned his wiring and came into the auditorium – *"Jason's fallen off the ladder"* cried Steve. A few moments later, Matt and I came to investigate – Jason was putting in an excellent performance, worthy of an Oscar itself. It was then that we all realised that the ladder had actually slipped and Jason really had fallen on to the auditorium seating, breaking his leg and injuring something else in the process! His injuries were so bad, an ambulance was called and it was Neville who had to dispatch the ambulance! Jason was taken off to A and E, leaving Matt to call his dad to break the news – *"Dad, its Matt. Jason has fallen off a ladder and been taken to hospital."* said Matt. *"Yeah, Very f*****g funny"* came the reply and the phone went dead! I've never had an April Fools Day story to challenge that one.

Each year, Aldeburgh Cinema played a vital part in the world famous Aldeburgh Festival, when all manner of 'arty-farty' folk ascended on the town and spent two weeks travelling between the concert hall at Snape and various other venues – the cinema being one of them – to enjoy a selection of specialist, archive and often obscure films. Many of these films would be screened in 16mm and Aldeburgh had a splendid German Zeiss 16mm projector, which Neville was very proud of and which had been adapted by the clever elders in the projection room. I never did like operating this particular projector and always referred to it as 'The Bitch', as whenever I operated the bloody thing, something would always go wrong.

There was a special screening of an old 16mm film, as part of the Aldeburgh Festival one Sunday afternoon, which would play to a full house. As I remember it, there had been some trouble with the delivery of the film and it didn't arrive until the afternoon of the day before. I was in the projection room with Neville and together, we checked the fragile film for any tears, repairing as necessary and it was to be Neville who thankfully was going to be responsible for running this film on the following day.

Sunday came and the telephone rang - it was Mrs. Gifford calling. Neville had been rushed into hospital and I was the only person available to show the film. *"Oh shit"* I thought, but declared *"No problem"* to Mrs Gifford, before hanging up the phone and counter-calling *"oh shit"* once again!

And so the afternoon came. A packed house was eagerly waiting below for the film to start. I had checked and double checked the film and was nervously waiting as the film was introduced. There was a round of applause and with that, I dimmed the house lights, started the projector, opened the picture on to the screen and checked the focus – all was well – well for at least two minutes, until the film suddenly snapped, turning the screen white. I stopped the projector, fixed the tear and restarted the equipment. A few minutes later and the film snapped again. And so this scenario went on – the film would snap, I would repair it and we'd start again.

After five or six breaks, the projection door opened and in stormed Mrs. Gifford. *"What on earth is going on"* she asked in a stern manner. My sweaty head appeared over the projector and in a firm tone I stated that *"I'm doing my best Mrs. Gifford."* The lady retreated and within a few seconds, the film was running again and I noticed that there was so much tape over the various joins in the film and that whenever one passed through the projector 'gate' it would force it open, thus causing the film print to snap. I then spent the following hour with my index finger firmly pressed against the gate, preventing it from springing open and allowing the show to continue.

At the end of the film, there was a round of applause – not for my finger, but for the film, although my finger was taking a well earned bow behind the porthole, in recognition of the position it had spent the past hour in. Needless to say, I politely refused to operate the 16mm projector again – the bitch!

I spent three very enjoyable years at Aldeburgh, working alongside some real characters and sharing a lot of laughs in the process. This was the venue that had instilled my passion for the art of showing films and Neville Parry was the best tutor any trainee could have encountered. I was happy in my work, but things were about to change – whether this was for the better remained to be seen.

"I see that Leiston are advertising for an assistant manager" said Susan Harrison, who was the office and front-of-house manager at Aldeburgh Cinema. This was either an observation that she thought may help me move forward, or she wanted to get rid of me – I could never work out which one! I grabbed the Suffolk Advertiser when I got home and she was right – Leiston Film Theatre had a vacancy

for a full time 'assistant to the manager'. I asked my father what he thought, to which he replied *"You'll never get any further down there"*. I was happy at Aldeburgh Cinema but I realised that my talents would never progress further than the projection room and I also knew that I had a lot more to offer. I decided I would apply for the advertised job and if all else failed; I would carry on showing the films at Aldeburgh.

I received a reply from the Town Clerk, Bob Morris, inviting me to attend an interview and offering me the opportunity to look around the Film Theatre prior to my appointment. I accepted this offer and on arriving at the Film Theatre, was greeted by the manager Peter Free, who proceeded to show me the foyer, box office, auditorium and stage – and that was it. No tour of the first floor or projection room – it was almost as if he didn't want to take me upstairs – it was his private area. I continued down the road to the Council Chambers, where I was interviewed by the Councillors Lew Howard, Trevor Hawkins and Lenny Neale, along with the Town Clerk Bob Morris. My intention was to be as frank and open as possible – they would ask me a question and I would give them a frank and honest answer – no bullshit – just tell them as it is. The way I saw it, I was merely there for a discussion – I was not desperate to get this job as I enjoyed my work at Aldeburgh. And so the interview was conducted – questions were asked, answers were offered, problems were posed, and solutions were resolved. And there it was – the interview was over. Hands shaken, I made my way home, feeling very confident with the way things had gone and 45 minutes later, Bob Morris was at my door with a letter offering me the job. I considered the offer thoroughly over the weekend and decided to go for it.

But before I officially accepted the offer, I had to break the news of my departure to Mrs. Gifford and I was dreading it - she had been very good to me and I respected her. The morning came – I had finished all my duties and so I ventured upstairs, past Harry and into the office to hand in my notice. A few moments later, I retreated, having done the deed, back down the stairs – avoiding the snappy

Jack Russell en route! In two weeks time, I would be showing my final film at Aldeburgh - I had big changes ahead.

" *A lovely cinema. Lovely staff and a fantastic local facility. Always a lot of thought put into accommodating children and great offers too. Myself and my children look forward to visiting Leiston Film Theatre.* **"**

Unbelievable

On Monday 25th May 1992, I walked into Leiston Film Theatre as its assistant manager and was once again greeted by Peter Free, who immediately introduced me to the cleaner, Pauline Clarke, who he would often refer to as *"a good ol' gal."*

Pauline had worked at the Film Theatre since 1982, when her mother-in-law stepped down from the post and was very welcoming and it soon became apparent that she was a thoroughly lovely lady – as Suffolk as could be – a motherly figure – you could easily find yourself confiding in her whenever you were annoyed about something or had a personal problem. She was often at the cinema for most of the morning, as a string of visitors would call in for a chat – her sister-in-law Velda, followed by her daughters – Dawn, Sarah and Kate, then the grandchildren and so it went on. If they were all going out together, they'd all turn up and join forces to help mum get away early – they were a rowdy lot when they all got together! Pauline stepped down as cleaner in 2012, having completed 30 years of service.

My tour of the venue continued with a stroll around the auditorium, dressing rooms and snack bar – which was basically a small counter, with three shelves selling cans of coke, which Peter would buy from the Gateway store in Sizewell Road, a box of polo mints and a Max-Pax drinks dispenser, which leaked more water than was ever used to make the out of date teas and coffees. As for the 'ticket office', this was literally a cupboard, with a stable style door with metal grill, from where the tickets were sold, with a wooden draw which was used to store the money – no cash tills anywhere! It was like stepping back in time, but the biggest shock was about to come.

You may recall that on the morning of my interview, Peter had escorted me around the ground floor, but didn't offer me the opportunity to view the first floor area. Well, after my demonstration on how to display six cans of coke, without letting the customer see the 'multipack' banner on the top of the tin, it was time to venture upstairs. The door was opened and I followed Peter up a narrow cast iron spiral staircase that made a worrying clanking sound. *"This has been here since day one"* said Peter and as we reached the top, he pointed to the wording 'Hayward Brothers Union Street Borough London', which was moulded into the ironwork on the top step. After 18 careful steps I'd reached the place that time had forgot – or that the owners had neglected and one honest thought came immediately to mind – *"what the hell have I done?"*

How on earth could anyone work in such poor conditions? Health and safety would have shut the place down without hesitation. The plastered walls and ceilings were falling apart, with large holes here and there. The flooring was torn, resulting in many a trip. There were two small rooms to the right at the top of the stairs. The first used to be the directors room, complete with a small hatch door, into what is the rear of the auditorium, from where you could look out into the theatre. The second room had been used as a rewind room and was completely lined out with tin, which was literally nailed to anything and everything – walls, floor, cupboards and rewind bench! The heavy and, where exposed, sharp tin was the remainder of the days of the highly flammable nitrate film, which was the cause of many fatal cinema blazes in the early 1900's.

We ventured into what Peter referred to as 'the office', but in reality, was no more than a dirty store room, filled with boxes, film posters and a knackered wooden bureau with draws that wouldn't open and a broken leg, which resulted in a rocking motion when anything touched it. On top of the desk was an old typewriter – Peter's mothers I believe – the ink had run dry and the metal arms would stick together if you tried to use it. There was also a very clean answer-phone machine – *"We've only had that for a couple of weeks"* Peter explained. A large rectangular table was located in the centre of the room and this was covered in a huge pile of papers.

Everything, and I mean everything, was covered in a seriously thick layer of dust. It was an absolute disgrace and an area that council officials probably hadn't ventured into in a very, very long while.

Now do you see why I was so convinced that I had made a grave error in career judgement? I had just left a cinema four miles down the road, which had just been installed with a new sound system, was in good decorative order and had comfortable working conditions. I wouldn't say that Leiston Film Theatre was entirely derelict, but even the fleas had left the pit!

A door opposite was unlocked and Peter led me into the projection room, which was again entirely lined with tin, with metal shutters located above the projection portholes, which remained from those dangerous nitrate days and would have been closed by pulling a metal chain, to contain a fire in the case of an emergency.

Peter proceeded to share various tales of his time in the projection room – the days when the projectionist was working continuously from the first frame of film until the curtains closed at the end of the credits. The 35mm reels would have been shown in 20 minute spools from reel 1, 2, 3 and so on – until the reels ran out, which in some cases could be up to 12 reels or more. Each reel would have a 'foot' or 'tail' on one end of the reel and a 'head' or 'leader' at the start – where a series of numbers are printed on the film in one second intervals from 11 to 3 – but only to 3, as the frames become black before the reel starts. The reel would be 'laced' through the projector and on to an empty collection reel beneath, with the number 8 positioned in the projector's 'gate'. Just prior to the start of the film, two carbon rods (one positive and one negative) would be lit and when positioned to burn in line with each other, a bright light would be produced and reflected by a curved mirror at the back of the projector housing, flooding the projector head with light and thus creating the image on the screen. The carbon rods had to be monitored regularly and swiftly adjusted if their angle altered, otherwise the brightness of the projected image would become faded. While one reel was playing, the previous one would be rewound in the rewind room and the next reel would be laced through the second projector – once again with number 8 in the projector gate – not forgetting to check those carbons! As the end of one reel approached, the second set of carbons would be lit and positioned. Next, the projectionist would stare through the projection room 'porthole', turning his full attention to the screen. In the last few seconds of the reel, a black 'motor' dot would appear in the top right hand corner of the screen – this was the projectionist's cue to start the second projector. Then, approximately eight seconds later a second black 'changeover' dot would appear, leaving one second of film remaining and this was the cue to switch the picture and sound from one projector to the other. Lacing the reel on number 8 would enable the end and start of each reel to meet in each projector gate, with no loss of film for the audience. This procedure would then be repeated at the end of each reel, throughout every performance – this was when a projectionist really did run the show. Of course, there were many times when the film would tear when starting the projector for the 'cross-over' and Peter would often recall the cheers and stamping of feet that could be heard coming from the auditorium until the problem had been resolved. The Film Theatre had operated on this basis until 1988 when the new projection equipment was installed.

Ahead of me was the brand new Cinemeccanica Victoria 8 35mm projector and platter system, often referred to as a 'cake-stand' due to its tiered construction. Having been used to changing film reels every hour at Aldeburgh, it was quite exciting to experience using the platter system which was quite simple – with this system, the film reels would be 'spliced' together in order of screening – reels 1, 2, 3 and so on and when the entire show of adverts, trailers and film had been loaded on to one of the platters, the front (or head) of the film would be fed through a 'feeder' plate, which would govern the speed at which the 'feeder' platter turned. The film would then leave the platter, travel along a number of wall mounted rollers, laced through the various workings of the projector itself, before returning to the cake stand, where it would be gathered on the 'collection' platter and a number of tension rollers would govern the speed at which the collection platter turned. It was clever stuff and providing that the film had been put together properly, was almost trouble free.

I was looking for a row of buttons to operate the masking. *"Where are the buttons for the curtains?"* I asked. *"There's no buttons here, just this handle."* said Peter and he pointed to a large winding handle attached to the wall, with steel wires running up into the tinned ceiling – as installed in 1935. A demonstration followed as I watched Peter turn the handle and the stage curtains opened to reveal the screen. *"Because they drag on the stage, you have to open them past the picture and then bring them back in."* he continued and it was noted that there were two thick strips of black material on the inner edge of the curtains, which acted as the masking for the film. The only problem was that, as these dragged on the floor, they had a tendency to angle outwards at the bottom.

At Aldeburgh, I would have just pressed a button and this would have been done for me.

I had walked into the building at 9am and at 11am Peter declared *"Well, that'll do us for now. I better get off and get a bit of grub and I'll see you tonight at 7pm."* And that was it - I got in my car and went home – covered in dust! At 2pm the phone rang – it was David Gooderham, the trainee Town Clerk. *"Where are you?"* he asked. *"At home. Peter said to come in tonight at 7pm"* I replied. *"Well you better get yourself back over here"* came the abrupt response – and so I did! The words 'piss-up' and 'brewery' sprang to mind and it was quite obvious that there appeared to be no 'plan' of what to do with their assistant manager and it was confusing for me to know who was actually in charge – Peter or the Town Clerk?

I spent that afternoon creating and photo-copying hundreds of programmes – not on a computer, but using that transfer lettering – the same that I had when I had my cinema in the shed. This was a difficult task in itself, as they only knew two films that were screening, as most films were programmed a few days ahead of showing at Leiston, with hardly any time to promote the film. Anyhow, I created a reasonable effort to promote the limited film programme and promptly distributed these around the town.

I returned to the Film Theatre just prior to 7pm for my first evening at Leiston Film Theatre. Peter introduced me to the two female members of staff who were working that evening and I proceeded to welcome the small sprinkling of customers (single figures) who came in to see *Star Trek: The Undiscovered Country*, which I had just finished showing a few days earlier in Aldeburgh! At 7.30pm, as Richard Clayderman played '*Any Dream Will Do*', Peter ventured upstairs and started the film. That was the only CD that Peter would play – Richard Clayderman and James Last – I still have it in my memory box. He would press the play button just before unlocking the doors at 7pm and he knew that it was exactly 7.30pm when that certain tune played. I suffered this CD during every shift for two years and have had a dislike for Richard Clayderman ever since.

Once the main film had started, the staff would cash up and then Peter would utter the words *"You might as well get yourself away"* and with that, the girls would collect their belongings and leave – and the best bit was that Peter would let them put 10pm on their timesheet! This procedure happened on a nightly basis and after a few evenings witnessing this, I asked Peter why the staff were allowed to go before the film ends. *"Well they've got boyfriends, or like to go out, or have to babysit on a Sunday night."* I couldn't believe it – staff were being paid to go babysitting and we were quite clearly breaching numerous regulations in the process.

David Gooderham and I entered into our roles within weeks of each other around the same time – I was at the Film Theatre and he was about to take over from a retiring Bob Morris as the new Town Clerk. David had worked for Leiston Urban District Council since 1953 as a rent collector, before covering as Leiston Town Clerk for a year in 1973 and then working at Suffolk Coastal District Council in Woodbridge from 1974 as a Committee Clerk. I always found David to be highly organised and never one to be piddled about by anyone.

He had a friendly but direct nature and whenever the time arrived for a gentle reprimand – which thankfully was few and far between, it was usually a lot of fuss over nothing – like the time when Joan Girling complained about me telling her to stop the children running around the auditorium during a Bright Sparks rehearsal! I was more concerned about one of the children tripping and knocking their head against the metalwork on one of the 292 seats, or one of the eight cast iron radiators. Anyway, I was ticked-off about this, although I didn't realise at the time. You see, David had a knack of delivering his slap-on-the-wrist and it was only when you left the office that you realised that you had received a polite but firm ticking-off. He didn't need to be arsy – his approach did the trick quite sufficiently. I still believe that I was in the right about those children though! David was always grateful when a job was done well and was quickly on the telephone, or at his word processor, with words of praise – that's the kind of gentleman David was.

David was thankfully in favour of the Film Theatre and would support and encourage wherever possible. He was able to nurture the council through some vital decisions and explaining the pros and cons of every matter in a way that assisted the councillors in making the right decisions.

As the weeks rolled on and my 'training' slowly progressed, it was becoming very apparent that the council had little idea, if any, of what was going on in their cinema and that it was little wonder that the place was stigmatised locally as a flea-pit. The decor was dated, the fixtures were shabby and above all else, the manager was just going through the motions, without any enthusiasm or initiative. It pains me to say this, but that's exactly how it was – Peter was a lovely, gentle man, but he was not a man of authority.

Peter was a very popular character in the town and everybody knew him. I liked him. This seems like a good place to tell you a little about Peter Free, who was manager at the Film Theatre from 1964, prior to the Town Council purchasing the cinema in 1976 and until he retired in 1994. Peter's father Albert, but more familiarly known as Toby, joined the Picture House in 1916 as an apprentice, where he worked as a 'Cinematograph Operator' (projectionist) and Peter's mother, May, was the cashier.

Peter always said that he couldn't remember his first time at the cinema, as he spent so much time there as a child, sitting on the cash till with his mother and would help his father in the projection room at the age of six. Indeed, we always laughed and remarked that he was probably conceived in the projection room! During the Second World War, Toby went to work at the local water works and Peter started officially working in the projection box, when the cinema was packed out every night. After national service in Greece, Peter took a job at the Regal cinema in Littleport and later, at the Exchange at Dereham. When his father died in 1957, aged 56 years, Peter returned to Leiston Picture House, first as a projectionist and then, from 1964 as the manager and later, as one of the directors, prior to the council buying the venue in 1976.

It was upon his return to Leiston, that Peter enrolled an 11 year old Allan Bayley, who would spend Saturday mornings pasting up posters around the town and oiling the projectors and then at the age of 15 and quite unlawfully, Allan would help out upstairs in the evenings, by rewinding the film reels, albeit balanced on a box, as he was too short to reach the rewind bench and was even running the films by himself by the time he turned 16.

Allan would spend many hours working alongside Peter and always remembers him as a man who *"loved the Picture House, loved the bookies, loved a bike ride and loved his cats."* And it was he who took great care of Peter when he was poorly towards the end of his life. Allan retired from the Film Theatre in 2011, with the introduction of the digital projection equipment, having completed 50 continuous years of service.

Joan Girling had been elected to the Town Council in May 1991 and within weeks of my appointment as assistant manager, she and David started to push forward notions to improve the cinema and a working party, comprised of nominated councillors would draw up a list of works required to maintain and enhance the building. In the company of David, Peter and myself, the venue was extensively explored – poking this and pulling that and after a detailed analysis, it was decided that the first items on the list should be the redecoration of the front exterior – this would mean having the entire front covered in scaffolding and obviously dealing with any rotten timbers prior to redecoration. It was considered paramount that the top of the front fascia should remain painted exactly as it was originally intended – in black and white – as it is today. Upstairs, a recommendation was made that the two small rooms at the top of the spiral staircase could be altered into one larger room and that the front office was in urgent need of redecoration – that was an understatement! The projection room was next – the metal sheeting, which was attached to everything would be removed, including a redundant air vent from the old projectors, which allowed rainwater to leak through whenever there was heavy rainfall – a bucket was always on hand just in case! It was also decided to recommend enlarging the projection room, by removing a partition wall and extending into a redundant store room. Downstairs, the ticket office was considered in need of updating and then, venturing into the auditorium, the obvious 'delicate' condition of the walls was observed – the hessian wall coverings were dirty and torn, with large cracks across many of the 1981 murals. The ceiling was seriously stained from years of tobacco smoke and it was obvious that considerable redecoration was required, with my idea of using drapes to the top half of the walls and a decorative wall covering to the bottom, appearing to prove a popular solution with those present – although careful consideration would have to be given to any final colour scheme.

There were six suspended Art-Deco glass chandeliers hanging from the auditorium ceiling. The option of replacing these with safer and more contemporary 'flush' fittings was contemplated before the cinema inspectors moved on to the matter of a solitary table and chair located on the top of an area above the double entrance doors at the rear of the auditorium. *"That's where Stephen does the lights"* explained Peter - this table was used to operate the lighting for live shows and was accessible via a creaking vertical ladder. An intake of breath demonstrated that this practice was most unsafe and that some form of partition should be erected to make this area safe to use. Onwards towards the screen and it was noted that the only

75

way to get on stage from the auditorium was to use a chair to access a side door that led to the 'wing' of the stage – various options were discussed and it was decided to recommend that some kind of stairs be somehow installed to make access easier and safer.

It was a comprehensive shopping list that needed to be prioritised, with an estimate of costs and a timescale to budget to – something that required a thorough structural survey and although this expenditure didn't sit comfortably with all councillors, it was passed at the vote and that duty eventually fell upon Frank Bilton of Hollins Architects in Framlingham – a tall, well spoken gentleman, who wore his trousers high and knew of all things structural but nothing about all things cinema. We always got on well and I think he could sense my frustration and aspirations for the cinema. Between us, we came up with a plan of works that would not only repair the cinema, but would also develop it – but of course, these improvements wouldn't happen overnight.

In fact, Hollins report wasn't presented to the Town Council until April 1993 – two years later and was, as you would expect, very thorough and generally summarised that the building was reasonably sound, although maintenance had been badly neglected and that it was in need of urgent decoration and repair to preserve the structure. Minutes from a three hour council meeting in April 1993, show the members acknowledging the poor programme of maintenance at the Film Theatre and a positive desire to restore the building, albeit that this task was going to be extremely costly.

Therefore, admission prices were promptly increased to £3.00 and £2.00 – the first increase for two years. It was going to take far more than an additional 10p price increase to raise the funds to unlock the potential of this Film Theatre, so hire charges were also increased – and then promptly reduced for Sunday mornings – of course, electricity and gas were cheaper at the weekend!

So, back to the story. In the meantime, I had to do my best to increase awareness of the venue and its programme and entice an increase in revenue. You had to tread carefully where Peter and the community as a whole were concerned. A lot of people feared change and the cinema had obviously been part of Peter's life for so many years. I knew that I would have my work cut out ahead of me and if the old place was to be a success again, then the first place to start was the snack bar – but this was far easier said than done where Peter was concerned.

On my evenings off, I would often visit the newly opened five screen Odeon cinema in Ipswich to catch the latest films. I loved the Odeon, Ipswich – it was what I considered a proper cinema – not too large, with comfy seats, great surround sound, curtains that opened and closed and the all important shop, where you could stock up on popcorn, ice creams and the like. It wasn't a trip to the movies and still isn't, without a tub of popcorn to crunch away on during the adverts and trailers. As I've already said, Leiston's 'snack-bar' boasted a leaking Max-Pax machine, half-a-dozen cans of coke, polo's (which the children used to enjoy throwing around the auditorium) and Walls' ice cream – but no popcorn. In order to generate an increase in revenue, we firstly needed to increase the selection of confectionery and drinks available, but Peter was quite adamant. *"We don't need popcorn – that stuff makes a mess!"* I would try to politely debate his statement, but he was firm on this stance – there was to be no popcorn.

I felt frustrated. Why had I been employed and what was I supposed to do? I explained my situation with David and after a fair bit of discussion, it was ultimately decided that David would raise me £100 of petty cash to visit the cash and carry in Ipswich, to purchase a selection of stock items to sell in the snack bar. With the cash in my hand, I spent an afternoon buying up bags of sweets, cases of drinks and boxes of popcorn!

I returned to the Film Theatre and eagerly stocked up the snack bar, ready for the next big film, but when Peter walked in and saw what I'd done, he was clearly annoyed and this was the first and only time I heard him swear. *"I told you I didn't want any f*****g popcorn."* he said bluntly, before stomping off upstairs to put the Richard Clayderman CD on. However, after a few days of brisk business (we were now into double figures), we had sold out of popcorn and I will never forget Peter coming through the double doors, grinning and claiming that *"I reckon they must sprinkle that stuff with crack – one bloke has just come back for another bag."*

Mission accomplished. However, this was just the start and it was a frustratingly lengthy process waiting for more petty cash to be raised at the monthly council meetings. A far cry from today, where we spend thousands of pounds on stock without any concern. Our movie munchies stand is a very important part of our business – not only does the income generated from this area keep the cinema ticket prices low, but it is where most smaller cinemas, including ourselves, subsidise our enormous running costs. Yes, our sweets may be a little more expensive than a supermarket – which is able to price their confectionery low due to their considerable buying power, but in buying a bucket of popcorn, slush drink, or even a cup of tea, you are directly helping to keep the Film Theatre open. Remember that next time you bring a carrier bag of sweets into our cinema and then leave your wrappers on the floor for us to clear up!

I'd only been working at the Film Theatre for six months when something happened to Peter that well and truly broke the ice between us both and put the popcorn saga behind us. This was my first experience of the annual Royal British Legion Festival of Remembrance – a chaotic evening where people were everywhere and nobody honestly knew what they were doing! In 1992, it was the done thing to have a table located in the foyer and for the Legion and band members to donate prizes for the draw as they arrived – a bottle of bubble bath, a tin of biscuits or if they were really lucky, a box of chocolates. The raffle was always drawn during a break in the second half and with ice creams sold, Peter and I retreated to the safety of the projection room, where Peter stood poised with his tickets in hand, ready to scoop a tin of peaches or a wilting pot plant. *"And now it's time for the draw"* said compère John Day and on cue, Peter would raise the house-lights, while the audience fiddled about, trying to remember where they'd put their tickets.

And so the draw began – *"Yellow ticket, 321"* or whatever and it went on and on and on. *"This'll go on forever"* said Peter, checking his numbers, as the tin of pineapple chunks was handed out, followed by a pot of custard powder. Peter chuckled as the collection of crap prizes was handed out, muttering the odd *"Unbelievable"*. Next came a tin of cat food and then the ray of light that was a pint of milk! The penny dropped and making a bolt for the projection room door, Peter declared *"Hang on a minute, that's my bloody shopping!"* You see, when Peter had arrived, he'd placed his bag of shopping under the draw table and some fool had presumed that the items had been donated to the raffle. By the time Peter had reached the back of the auditorium, the shopping had gone – all gone, even the gravy granules! Peter raced down to the front of the stage, explaining his predicament to John Day, who proceeded to share the incident with the audience, much to everyone's great amusement. To top it all, the lucky recipients of Peter's shopping offered to return the goods, but Peter being Peter said *"No, you won it, you keep it."* I cried with laughter, Peter cried with laughter and the story has been reminisced at the Festival of Remembrance ever since. Thankfully, these days the prizes have improved and no longer includes the handouts of the audience.

In November 1992, a group of people, including myself and headed by – you guessed it – Joan Girling, arranged a meeting with a view of forming a 'friends' of the Film Theatre. This initial meeting was attended by a gathering of willing volunteers, all passionate about their local cinema and with John Farmer in charge as Chairman, various ideas were explored as to how they could help promote and improve the Film Theatre. During the early days of the Leiston Film Theatre Support Club, as it became known, funds were raised to support the purchase of smaller items, but attention would eventually be drawn to major projects in future years, that would have a direct impact on the operation of the venue.

I had only been in my new job for a number of months when I met with the Town Clerk and suggested that, rather than he book the films – usually a few days before we played them, I should take on the role of film booker and produce a monthly programme. This is what the other independent cinemas had been doing for years, so why hadn't Leiston? David was enthusiastic about the idea and in the coming weeks, we both spent a day in London, trailing around the various film distributors – shaking lots of hands, making them aware that the council were now running the cinema again and that I would be responsible for booking the films.

Film distributors are a combination of characters and in my experience, are notoriously difficult to get hold of – highly frustrating when you have advertising deadlines approaching and really need to book that elusive film! These days, most bookings are conducted via email, with hardly a word spoken between the two parties and even now you still find yourself chasing them for an answer, but in the 1990's I was always on the phone trying to track down Sav from Twentieth Century Fox, or Bob from Warner Bros. These are two examples of the type of characters I dealt with. I genuinely hated having to phone Sav – trying to book a film with this guy was sheer hard work, as I would want a film from a certain date, but Sav wanted me to show it a week later and our conversation would often involve Sav offering the phrase *"Do you want the bloody film or don't ya?"*, whereas Bob was the complete opposite and without question, the nicest bloke I've ever done film business with – he was a helpful, polite and humorous chap – and it was Bob who allowed me to book my first film from its UK release date. The film in question was the 1993 family film *Dennis*, which was due for release on the first day of the schools summer break.

It had been a long time since Leiston had shown a film from release and Peter was concerned that I had committed the cinema to showing the film for two weeks (the minimum run for a film on release). At last I had something to get my teeth into. Posters and trailers were ordered and I embarked on spreading the news that *Dennis* was coming to town! This promotion included thousands of programmes being printed and distributed everywhere, from shop counters to telephone boxes and many mentions in the Suffolk Advertiser – a free weekly paper, which conveniently had an office at the bottom of the High Street, manned by Jackie Manning and Ray Grimmer, who were very supportive of my efforts to gather coverage for the Film Theatre – to the extent that in the week leading up to the release of *Dennis*, a review of the film was featured in the paper, declaring it as 'the family film of the summer'. It worked – the screenings of *Dennis* were a huge success and this gave us an opportunity to promote the other films that were showing at the Film Theatre and in the coming weeks, we did excellent business on the wet days, but we always suffer when the sun has got his hat on!

You see, unless you have a really, really big film, people are reluctant to go to the movies on a warm sunny day and we always notice that whenever the rain begins to fall, the phone starts to ring. We've had some summers when the weather has been so good, we may as well be closed during the day – they still come at night, but that doesn't help us during the day. I always like the weather to be fine on a Friday and Saturday, so that everyone can settle in their holiday accommodation (and so I can cut my grass) and then for it to piddle down Sunday to Thursday (so I can watch it grow!)

By this time I'd left home and was living at 81 High Street – conveniently opposite the Film Theatre and my relationship with my father had improved greatly. I now had my space and he had his – plus he was enjoying the benefit of a 10% discount on his Council Tax! He now had a new lady in his life – Jean, who had also lost her partner several years earlier and although I found this a difficult scenario to comprehend initially, they found companionship with each other and Jean made sure that my father wasn't going to become an idle widower and shut himself away after his bereavement.

I was suddenly realising the power of the press in spreading the word and in the coming months, I concocted a number of exaggerated 'tales' to entice the column centimetres! Like when we played *Home Alone 2: Lost in New York* for Christmas 1993. We had worked hard to promote this film for the school holidays and were rewarded with full houses for many of the showings – to the extent that I became aware that we'd taken more money with the film, than they had at The Plaza in Regent Street. The report in the East Anglian Daily Times, complete with a large photo of me and

Peter, clutching a tub of popcorn and a cardboard cut-out of Macaulay Culkin between us, did state that *"A surprised spokesman from the Plaza confirmed the figures and said that other West End cinemas had shown the film before them, which may have affected their audience figures."* Precisely, but who cared. Spotting this fact and manipulating it to our advantage had made the news and provided several more packed screenings before we finished playing the film.

As 1993 continued, I managed to obtain more of the big films quickly – films like *Mrs. Doubtfire*, *The Fugitive*, and *Shindlers List*, but getting hold of *Jurassic Park* was an absolute nightmare. You see, the film was distributed by UIP and my contact, Nigel, always had to ask the sales director, Peter, if we could show the film before Aldeburgh. He would literally put the phone on his desk and I would hear him ask Peter if we could show the film. In the instance of *Jurassic Park*, Aldeburgh were not showing the film until week seven, so we couldn't play the film until week eight. This was highly frustrating for me and so I produced hundreds of leaflets promoting the fact that we would not be increasing our ticket prices for Jurassic Park – as many cinemas had, due to the ridiculously high rental terms for this particular film and with the help from Jackie and Ray at the Suffolk Advertiser, the film was a complete success, but nowhere near as busy as if we'd been allowed to show it a lot earlier.

Then there was the time when we were showing the 'erotic thriller' *Body of Evidence*, in which Madonna drips candle wax all over Willem Dafoe in a steamy sex scene. The film was not doing good business, probably because it was bloody awful, but thankfully it was running on top of Disney's re-release of *The Jungle Book*, which was filling the cinema in the afternoons. Customers were walking out, apparently appalled by Madonna's acting skills – one such walker was local resident Pete the Greek, who abandoned the film declaring it as *"a load-a sheet"* (I've tried to write this in my best Greek accent!) And so, after a weekend of 'walkers', I casually strolled into the neighbouring office of the East Anglian Daily Times and let it drop that customers had been walking out 'shocked' at the sex scenes. On cue, the reporter appeared with notepad in hand and the following day, I opened the paper to see a photo of a half naked Madonna and the headline *"Madonna film too steamy for Leiston cinema-goers."* This resulted in a brilliant Tuesday, Wednesday and Thursday night and the funniest bit was when Pete the Greek crossed the street a few days later to make it quite clear to me that *"I no walk-outta da film coz i-wazza shock ad -da zex. I walk-outta coz id-za load a-sheet."* I have never forgotten those words.

It was dead handy having the East Anglian Daily Times office next door. They rented the shop from the council and a reporter was always on hand if I had a story to tell – which I always did.

Later in the year, we made the news again – press, radio and even the television, when we successfully overturned the film classification of the 1993 Robin Williams comedy *Mrs. Doubtfire* from a 12 classification, to a PG. The film had been granted a 12 certificate by the British Board of Film Classification, due to a series of sexual references which were considered to be unsuitable for a PG film and one scene in particular, where Mrs. Doubtfire questions his ex-wife's new boyfriend about his intentions towards her. In the film, Mrs. Doubtfire states *"A man gives a present like that he wants more than a piece of her heart...bit of a going-down payment, huh? You know dear, sink the sub? Hide the weasel? Park the porpoise? Bit of the old humpty dumpty? Little Jack Horny? The horizontal mambo? The bone dance, eh? Rumpleforeskin? Baloney bop? Bit of the old cunning linguistics? Hmm?...* and so it goes on.

The phone rang and it was Trevor Wicks from the Hollywood Cinema in Lowestoft. *"Are you planning to challenge the rating for Mrs. Doubtfire? I am. They're watching the film tomorrow and I'm hoping they'll reduce it from a 12 to a PG."* This was news to me, but Trevor explained that the local authority – in our case, Suffolk Coastal, had the powers to alter a films certificate if it were considered to be inappropriate. I spoke to David and it was decided that we too would challenge the film's classifications – not for the sake of appropriate content, but for the sake of publicity and the cash tills! And so we did, the licensing authority at Suffolk Coastal District Council watched the film and agreed that the 12 certificate was indeed inappropriate and could be amended to a PG. Trevor and I were on the news – and the newspaper – and the radio, spouting on about how it was a family film and that the family could not watch it ... blah, blah, blah. We gained so much publicity that people were travelling from all over the county to watch the film in Leiston and we enjoyed many packed houses as a result.

Much later, in 2002, the 12 classification was replaced with the now familiar 12A certificate, whereby children under 12 may be admitted to a 12A film, providing that they are accompanied by an adult, aged at least 18 years of age.

Such coverage had proved that an audience was out there. It was merely a case of getting the message across that there was a cinema in Leiston (you'd be surprised how many people didn't realise that the venue existed) and that we successfully advertised the programme.

1: The front exterior in 1914.
2: The interior of the hall in 1914 - there are actually five people sitting in the 'orchestra pit'.
3: An interior view from the stage in 1914 - there was no rear partition at this time - this was added in 1933. Bundles of seats are stacked on the hall floor awaiting installation.
4: Leiston Picture House manager, William. S. Hammick. He ruled the Picture House with regimental efficiency from 1915 until 1945.
5: Picture House director Ted Titlow (left) and manager William S. Hammick (right).

1980 - Leiston Town Council enrol the services of Chris Foster, who organised a group of volunteers to redecorate the Picture House auditorium - not my cup of tea, but very much part of the cinema's story. The murals became a permanent feature for 23 years until the major auditorium refurbishment in 2000.

1: No matter what the age, every volunteer was handed a paintbrush.

2: Once the base coat was applied, the artists moved in to create the film star murals.

3: A 47 year old Peter Free lends a helping hand in brightening up the drab auditorium.

4: The finished article - Hollywood icons Clark Gable and Marilyn Monroe look down on cinema-goers - other likenesses included Charlie Chaplin, The Beatles and even Peter Free himself!

Prior to the auditorium undergoing refurbishment in 2000. The walls were in a terrible condition, the exit curtains were filthy and the seating was torn, but Suffolk's oldest cinema was about to shake off its 'flea-pit' stigma and receive a new identity, thanks to the voluntary efforts of its management, staff and supporters. The new-look auditorium was completed in July 2001.

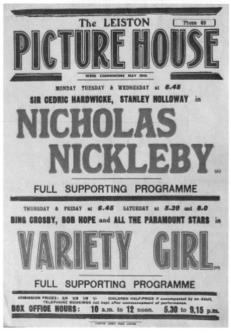

1: Elsie Fairweather unveils a memorial Picture House clock in 1978, in memory of the long serving Dr. Burlingham. 2: Peter Free 'lacing' the film through the projector before the start of another showing in 1988. Bottom: Picture House posters advertising the weekly programme from 1934 (left) and 1947 (right).

Grabbing the headlines!

1: Peter Free and I celebrate after taking more money than the Plaza in Regent Street with *Home Alone 2: Lost in New York* in 1992.

2: The BBFC 12 classification for *Mrs Doubtfire* was amended to a PG by our local authority, after we had successfully argued that the 12 rating was excessive, resulting in packed houses in 1994.

3: I receive a soaking from Sooty and Richard Cadell, who seriously injured his head during a performance in 2002 and Sooty became the only puppet to be barred from the Film Theatre!

Above: The Film Theatre team in 1994. L to R: Sara Lloyd, Darren Payne, yours truly, Peter Free, and Doreen Bailey (back row). Christina Brown, Pauline Clarke, Kate Clarke, Maria Bayley and Allan Bayley (front row). Below: Hannah Everett and I with the Film Theatre's centenary mascot, Cheeky the Centenary Chimp in 2013.

Above: Peter Free served as manager at the Film Theatre from 1964 until 1994 and is seen here in the projection room prior to the new projection and sound equipment being installed in 1988. The projection room remained lined with tin sheets, from the days of nitrate film, until refurbishment in 1998.
Below: The projection room as it is today. The 35mm platter system has been retained and stands beside the new digital 3D projector. Leiston Film Theatre Support Club continues to finance the repayments on a loan required to fund the digital equipment.

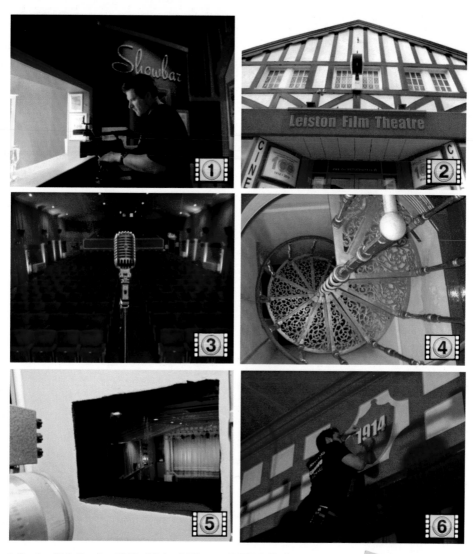

1: Sunday 13th October 2013 - Michael Gibson of MG Media devotes a marathon 14 hours capturing Leiston Film Theatre for a unique souvenir DVD to commemorate the venues centenary in 2014.

2: The front exterior was captured from all angles - even from 15ft above the venue itself!

3: An artistes view of the auditorium - one of my favourite images.

4: The original 1914 cast iron spiral staircase - redecorated in gold for the 100th anniversary.

5: A view from the projection room porthole.

6: The all important numbers 1914 are fitted to the original proscenium plaque.

The centenary souvenir DVD is available from Leiston Film Theatre ... ONLY £5.00

1: Posing in the projection room for a magazine article in 2005. 2: One of my first outings on the Film Theatre stage in 1996. 3: Stephen Ginger and I make final preparations on stage before the curtain goes up on another Bright Sparks pantomime - I'm the one on the left, just in case you are wondering!

Above: The fascia in 1994 - the Film Theatre's 80th anniversary - and it certainly looked it!
Below: Transformed, the fascia in 2013 - the striking new signage was installed in 2010.

My pride and joy. Our comfortable 300 seat auditorium in 2010. Since these wonderful photographs were taken, we've added the Showbar at the rear of the auditorium, an orchestra pit under the stage and have even more ambitious plans ahead during our centenary year.

A change of reel

It was March 1994 and Peter Free retired from Leiston Film Theatre, in the same year that his beloved cinema would celebrate its 80th anniversary. Well, when I say retired, I mean he stepped down as manager one day and then came in to cover for me on the following evening! We celebrated his 'retirement' with a surprise gathering of staff, councillors and Support Club committee members, following a day of performances by the Kay Goddard and Coral Stebbings dance schools. It had been a long day, but Peter was genuinely surprised by our efforts and was presented with a number of gifts – a painting of him on the front steps of the Film Theatre from the Support Club, a carriage clock from the Town Council and the Film Theatre staff had made a collection and in the coming weeks sent Peter and Allan off to London by train to visit the Museum of the Moving Image, followed by a tour of the Empire, Leicester Square.

Peter would stand in for me on a couple of nights each week, so that I could attempt to have a social life and although on the management hand-over, I had immediately replaced the Richard Clayderman CD with *Now That's What I Call Music 27*, Mr. Clayderman always found his way back into the CD player whenever I was away – no matter where I'd hidden him and even funnier, no words were ever exchanged over this between Peter and myself – we just continued swapping CD's, depending on who was working!

A few days after I officially became the manager of Leiston Film Theatre (April 1st actually!), I quickly arranged a staff meeting, insisting that all members of staff should attend, as there were changes ahead. Everyone arrived and I began by explaining that, with immediate effect, all members of staff would have to remain on duty until the film had finished and the building had been checked and secured – up until then, Peter had been letting the staff go home after they had cashed up and paying them until the end of the show. I explained that this had been a breach of our fire, safety and licensing conditions and that this couldn't continue to happen. Within a couple of weeks, I had lost two members of staff, who didn't approve of my new policies and these were swiftly replaced, with one of the new cashiers being a bubbly and curvaceous woman by the name of Christina Brown.

Christina was originally from Telford, Shropshire, but now lived in Knodishall and replied to an advertised vacancy for a cashier/ usherette. Christina was the ideal cashier – friendly, punctual, polite, helpful – I could go on, but I don't need to – she always put in a brilliant performance for the customers, no matter what was going on in her personal life – she called it her 'cinema face'. We got on very, very well and in her early days at the cinema, she apparently developed a 'thing' for me, or so she later told me after she'd got wise! Her husband, Peter, worked at the Sizewell B Power Station and we would often socialise together, sharing several antics during our working time together. It was Christina who would undertake the training of all new front-of-house staff, starting with the words *"Lose your gum, tuck yourself in and smile."* She would even stand in for me when I was away on holiday. If we were busy, I could simply look at her and she would know exactly what to do or say – she was perfect. She had a very naughty mind and very often, once the film had started of course, most conversations would feature the odd innuendo or two or three, or simply smutty talk of some kind. For example, I would innocently say *"That door is getting stiff"* and Christina would reply *"Lucky door!"* or something a lot ruder! She was genuinely passionate about her little cinema and would bring any relatives who travelled to stay with her and Peter to see where she proudly worked.

Christina always said that the fact that she worked at the Film Theatre for four years was a testament of how much she enjoyed her job – she had only been in most of her other jobs for a matter of weeks and she would have almost certainly been my first choice for

98

an assistant manager, but the pair decided to move back to Shropshire in 1999, which was a genuine shame and I was sad to lose not only a fine employee, but a cherished friend.

We remained friends long after she left the area however and I went to stay with them on a number of occasions, as did other members of the 'team' that she was part of. Christina became a proud mum to a long awaited baby Sam in July 2009 and shortly after was diagnosed with Cancer, which she so bravely fought, but to no avail and as her illness progressed, she organised a visit to Leiston, accompanied by Peter and a toddling Sam, whereby the few familiar faces of her cinema 'team' got together for an evening of memories – she even paid her cinema a visit and was amazed at all the alterations. Belinda, Katie and I travelled down to see her, a couple of weeks before she sadly passed away in November 2011, aged 41 years. We travelled down again to Telford a few weeks later for her funeral and I was sincerely touched to hear her times at the Film Theatre so fondly recalled during her eulogy.

Sam - before your mum passed away, she wanted some of her family and friends to write a few lines about her, so that she could put all those comments in a book for you to read when you are older. I promised your mum that, instead, I would write about her in this book and I want you to know that your mum was beautiful, kind, courageous and above all else, fun. She adored you Sam. Bill (Belinda) and I still remember her fondly – she was, as you may have gathered, lovely, and I hope that one day, when you are old enough, you will come and visit us at the Film Theatre, where your mum spent so many happy times.

It was around this time also that a young man made an enquiry about working at the Film Theatre as a projectionist. His name was Darren Payne – a tall, scrawny lad, with long hair, tied back with an elastic band. He told me that he had enquired elsewhere, but was turned away. Darren reminded me of myself – not that I was scrawny or had long hair you understand, but he wanted to be a projectionist just like I had. Mrs. Gifford had given me that chance and I felt almost obliged to give this young man the same opportunity. So I took him on for a trial basis, to see if he was suitable for the job, as some people just can't get to grips with the logistics of the job. I spent the best part of a month showing Darren the ropes – how to 'splice' the film together, how to 'lace' the projector and how to open those curtains with the handle to make them look automated! Within a few weeks, Darren had well and truly got 'it' and was soon running the equipment unsupervised and a very, very good job he did of it too.

He got on with most of the staff, especially Belinda and Christina and for a while, he was Christina's lodger. We had a lot of laughs, both in and out of work – it was a good time – I had a great team and Darren was there for four years, before his ambitions landed him a job as a projectionist at the brand new 11 screen Virgin cinema in Ipswich, which opened in May 1998. I was sorry to see Darren go, as he had been an excellent member of staff, but I couldn't help but also feel proud that the training he had received at Leiston had helped him on his career path. I genuinely wished him great luck. I didn't see Darren again until a few of us got together with Christina in 2011, although I'm hoping he'll come and see the old place sometime soon.

That's the thing about staff. They come and they go – most are a total credit to the venue and the odd one or two have been a complete pain in the arse. We've had some who stole money from us (and got caught) and one who was a little too handy with a webcam! Of course, they are all here to earn money, but I'd like to think that the majority of them have a genuine will to see the venue retained. Belinda Borrett is one of those people – she has worked at Leiston Film Theatre since 1995 and is the only remaining member of my original 'post-Free' team. She still works her regular Tuesday and Wednesday evenings and comes in to watch the film every Friday night – very much a creature of habit, a dear friend and a terrific employee – I would hate to lose her.

I dread to think how many staff have come and gone through the Film Theatre doors in my 21 years but one thing is for sure – they have all been characters and part of a unique family. There was the one who wore skirts so short, the ice cream sales went through the roof, as the lads kept buying Cornetto's, so they could watch her bend over the freezer! There was another that didn't take any nonsense from the customers and had to be reprimanded when she asked a gobby teenager *"Are you taking the piss? Do you want a smack in the mouth?"* and there was the projectionist who didn't want to stay behind and take the film apart and consequently removed his tee-shirt, told me to stuff my job and walked home half naked in the pouring rain!

I like to think that they all aim to offer a friendly, unrivalled level of customer service, with a smile and the manners that, in my experience, you simply don't get at most large multiplexes.

I knew we had to do something to celebrate the venue's 80th anniversary in 1994 – and get us in the news again! We were going to be showing the film *Speed* from its UK release date and we were granted permission to present a preview screening a few days before the film actually opened in the UK, to commemorate the venue's 80th birthday. Invitations were sent out to councillors, Peter, staff (existing and former) and numerous invited guests, including all the major film distributors (even Sav) and a couple of them actually bothered to come along – or perhaps more so to get out of the city for a night or two.

Peter didn't feel that this film was suitable viewing for the members of the Town Council. Just in case you don't know the plot, *Speed* was an action-packed, edge-of your-seat thriller, in which a crazed terrorist plants a bomb on a bus, which will detonate if the bus' speed drops below 50mph. Keanu Reeves starred as the maverick cop, who climbs on board the bus, falls in love with Sandra Bullock and ends up decapitating Dennis Hopper – with a lot of action and one-liners in-between. Thankfully, although not surprisingly, the film went down very well during the anniversary showing and was followed by a small reception at Leiston Leisure Centre, complete with buffet, drinks, birthday cake, speeches and plenty of mingling. The evening had been a complete success – my staff had done me proud and I was one very happy manager.

At the end of the night, a group of burley film distributors were left stranded, in need of a taxi to Aldeburgh, where they were staying. It was duly noted that they were not in London anymore and that they would find it difficult to hail a cab at the bottom of Red House Lane. I offered to drive them all to Aldeburgh in the back of my Ford Fiesta – to say it was cosy on the back seat, would be a complete understatement, as a slightly drunken conversation flowed between them on the four mile journey – mainly ideas on how I could improve the cinemas interior decoration – one comment being *"It looks 80 years old!"*, their forthcoming films and the odd remark about the taxi service of Suffolk. I dropped them off at their hotel, to words of appreciation and I drove back to Leiston, contemplating on what had been a successful night. Exactly how successful remained to be seen the following day when, on his way back to London, Ian Johnston, the Sales Director from Disney called to thank me for my hospitality and the lift to Aldeburgh. *"Let me know if I can do anything to say thank you."* he said and without hesitation I replied *"Well, how about if you let us play The Lion King from release?"* There was some mumbling on the other end of the phone and it was generally agreed that we could play the film 'on date', but that we'd have to have show it for four consecutive weeks!

You see, in 1994 the film distributors often stipulated lengthy runs for their films – okay if you're a multi-plex and can ship a poorly performing film to a smaller screen, but no good whatsoever, if you were a single screen cinema, so to commit our screen to a four week run, even if it was a Disney film, was a considerable gamble. There was the possibility that the film would have an enormous week during the October half term holidays, but may fall flat on its arse either side of the school break. Peter felt very uneasy with the entire idea, but the film had already been released in the US and was a *roaring* success (sorry, couldn't help myself), becoming the biggest film of the year and so we went for it – we played the film for four long weeks – breaking all our box office records and running out of the beloved popcorn in the process (now sold in boxes from a large warmer). It was a very exciting few weeks and with the building wrapped in scaffolding, as the roof was repaired and re-tiled, huge queues were stretching along the High Street on a daily basis and the 'SOLD OUT' sign was being brought out on many days – even if we weren't quite full – it got us in the paper! The only down side was that we soon tired of hearing the catchy songs, especially the toe-tapping *Hakuna Matata* – we knew the film inside out and even now, I can't stand to hear that bloody tune and I'd imagine that you're humming it right now!

It was incredible to think that in its 80th year, Leiston's cinema had packed them in once more and as a result, the balance sheet was showing a small profit.

And there was really good news to end what had been a wonderful year when in October 1994, a report by the Monopolies and Mergers Commission concluded that five major film distribution companies were acting unfairly towards independent cinemas – insisting that 'first run' films were shown for a minimum period of at least four weeks. Only a few months earlier, I had been offered *The Lion King* from its UK release date with a stipulation of a lengthy four week run – although this had been entirely successful, it did prohibit cinemas from playing smaller films until weeks after release, when a seven day run was permitted. In 1993, I wasn't allowed to screen *Jurassic Park* until Aldeburgh Cinema had played the film – effectively 'barring' us from showing the film until week eight of release. The report also addressed this issue and with this new order coming into effect from March 1997, it seemed that showing the latest films quicker was going to be a lot easier in the coming months.

I'm hoping that by now, you can see just how hard we were all working at turning the old place around. People were returning to their local cinema again, for the first time in years. *"I haven't been in here since Ben Hur!"* said one customer, with another enquiring *"Are the toilets still up the back?"* And many of these people lived in the town, less than a five minute walk away – *"Unbelievable"*, as Peter would have said.

In June 1995, we presented the first of a few ladies 'strip' nights –

you know the type of thing, a comedian or drag queen, two or three strippers and as it turned out – a full house and a healthy profit. The show in question was *The Ultimate Fantasy Show* – starring 'The Guys that Dare to Bare!' and singer/comedian/compère Neil Sands – a former wrestler – a nice chap, who in previous years had topped the bill against the likes of Kendo Nagasaki and Giant Haystacks and now, as a producer and performer, was about to take on the ladies of Leiston.

Tickets went on sale and in no time, the Leiston grapevine was vibrating in anticipation of the naked flesh that was coming town – even my staff (except for Darren) was excited and queuing up to work at the thought of catching a glimpse of 'striptease superstars' Billy Hot Rocks and Simon Santata Top Gun – there was another but I can't remember his name! We hardly had to spend any money promoting this show – the mothers in the school playground were doing that job for us.

And so the night came. Doors were unlocked and within a few moments, the street was filled with the sound of high heels and drunken cackles, as groups of slurring women, who had been enjoying a pre-show drink (or six) at The Black Horse, staggered into the theatre, threw sexual threats in my direction and took their seats. This was a first for me – I'd never experienced anything like it – a real eye-opener. The noise was incredible – and the show hadn't even started yet! Even the quietest of the ladies in the Co-op (the ones who came across as timid) were all over the shop and very randy – it was hilarious.

The show ran like this; the compère would do around 15 minutes, followed by the first stripper, who would 'perform' for 15 minutes, followed by a 20 minute break, whereby most of the audience would rush down to The Black Horse for another drink. Then, the same procedure would be repeated, only this time with stripper number two. A quick break – yes that's right, back down the pub again, returning in time to catch the third and final stripper.

The posters had claimed that they 'dared to bare' and they certainly did – one brought a shower on stage with him, another ran naked flames all over his body and all of them used copious amounts of baby oil – the stage was like a skating rink – so much so that poor Billy Hot Rocks did an oily backward flip, which resulted in him crashing to the stage – thankfully not on his 'equipment'. To riotous screams of *"Off, off, off"* they removed their naval, fireman and policeman costumes, to reveal their corresponding periscope, fire hose and truncheon.

And that was that. The show came to end, the ladies vacated the theatre – back to the pub no doubt and I ventured backstage to settle up. I knocked on the dressing room door, entered and quickly said *"I'll be back in a minute."* I had walked in on a 'private party' – the kind that had plenty of sausages, but without the sticks. It was obvious that some of the 'fans' had found their way to the rear dressing room door for an autograph, but had clearly forgotten their pens! Neil, who wasn't invited to the 'party' came and found me to collect the fee and after a quick chat and securing a date for another appearance, returned backstage to square-up with his randy cast. A while later, after they had all gone and I was securing the dressing rooms, collecting several empty baby oil bottles on my way, I couldn't help but notice a lot of small elastic bands all over the floor – *"So that's how they look so big"* I thought and with that I locked up and left a note for Pauline to wear her Marigolds when cleaning the dressing rooms on Monday and to dispose of all elastic bands!

In the following years, we enjoyed many other lucrative sell out performances by different visiting strip shows - those 'who dare to bare', and the 'masters of striptease'. In fact, they used every slogan you could think of. These shows were bizarre experiences - to sit and have a normal conversation with these men backstage before the show, while they quite happily sat and 'prepared' themselves for their performance was quite insane. Most of these men would do this job six nights a week – that's a lot of elastic bands and they clearly loved all the attention that they received from the hungry audience.

I had decided that, as refurbishment work was edging ever nearer to the crucial auditorium, it would be prudent to call it a day on these shows, but we would bow out with a bang – a really big striptease spectacular, but as things turned out, that show never made it to the stage, but more about this as we continue.

The 1995 local elections provided several new faces on the Town Council, with Joan Girling romping home with the majority vote and as the retiring Chairman, was keen to report that the venue had made its first profit since the council purchased the venue in 1976. She also indicated that although the Film Theatre was a vital amenity to the town, it was also a business and needed to operate as such – at last, somebody was singing from my sheet.

Within a few weeks, phase two of the Film Theatre refurbishment programme was immediately initiated, after an electrical inspection rendered the electrical wiring at the Film Theatre old and in urgent need of attention. The licensing department at Suffolk Coastal District Council provided (after negotiation) a six month window in which to action the necessary electrical works and the council had little alternative other than to take prompt action or risk having the venue closed. This provided us with an opportunity to make various improvements to the electrics at the Film Theatre – it really was almost as if we were rewiring the place for the first time. We could now position the various sockets and switches to more practical locations, replacing the 1935 suspended glass chandeliers in the auditorium, with 20 'flush' down-lighters in the process – all in symmetrical rows of course.

In the spring of 1996 and quite spontaneously, I applied for an advertised vacancy for an assistant manager at a triple-screen multiplex in Camberley, Surrey, which was part of the independent Robins Cinemas chain. The only reason that I had responded to the advertised position was the fact that I was struggling on my Film Theatre salary. The cinema in Camberley had recently been taken over by Robins Cinemas, from the Cannon group. The cinema was 64 years old and, as I remember, on one very sunny day, I travelled down to Surrey by train to take a look around the complex – and it was a lovely cinema, before heading into the city for my job interview, which was with Ben Freedman and was conducted in a swanky office, with Ben sitting on one large leather couch and me sitting opposite on another. The interview was very informal, as he told me all about Robins Cinemas and I gave him an education on Leiston Film Theatre. The discussion was going well and then I mentioned Mrs. Gifford and to my surprise, Ben knew of her – in fact, he was somehow very fond of her. After 30-or-so minutes, we shook hands and I returned home. I received a call the following day, advising me that I had been shortlisted for the job.

Whilst in Camberley, I had taken time to research the relevant costs of living in Surrey and it wasn't cheap – that was a problem. However, if I was successful in getting the job, I would be earning much more than I was being paid in Leiston – I was confused and so I paid the Town Clerk a visit and we had an open discussion about my situation. David didn't want to see me leave the Film Theatre and quickly brought this to the attention of the Town Council, who in consideration of the scenario gestured an immediate increase in salary. I did my sums and financially, I wouldn't have been any better off by moving to Surrey and so I decided to stay put at the Film Theatre and just as well, as the Robins cinema in Camberley closed in May 2003.

This was also the year when Peter Free really did retire from life at the Film Theatre. His family had been associated with the venue for all but two years of its trading life and he had served the town as their cinema manager for 30 continuous years – an 'unbelievable' achievement – through the Town Council purchase, then through the disastrous leasing fiasco, and then the arrival of an enthusiastic twenty-something who wanted to turn the place upside down! He handed his bunch of keys in, put his cycle clips on, peddled off down the High Street and would never set foot inside the Film Theatre again.

I wasn't about to let Peter ride off into the celluloid sunset without the obligatory publicity rounds in the local press. I even arranged for Peter to be interviewed live, as the special guest of Lesley Dolphin on BBC Radio Suffolk – chatting about his life at the cinema. I saw this as an ideal publicity vehicle to spread the word about Leiston Film Theatre and on the journey to the radio station in Ipswich, Peter wouldn't stop recalling tales from the projection room – everything seemed very good. Dressed in a suit (just in case somebody could see him on the radio) Peter took his seat in front of an intimidating microphone and while the preceding record was playing, Lesley made it quite clear that there was plenty of time and to feel free to be as detailed as he liked.

The song ended, a jingle was played and Lesley introduced Peter to the listening radio audience. *"So"* said Lesley, *"After all those years at Suffolk's oldest cinema, you must have seen a lot of changes over the years?"* There was a brief pause. *"Yes* (pause) *I have."* replied Peter. *"And it must be great to see the cinema still open?"* asked Lesley. There was another pause. *"Yes* (pause) *it is."* Despite being as chatty as could be on the way to Ipswich, Peter's answers consisted of nothing more than a *"yes"* here, a *"no"* there and after five-or-so minutes, poor Lesley politely thanked Peter for joining her and wished him a long and happy retirement. I mouthed *"sorry"* to Lesley as we left the studio and on returning to the car, Peter remarked *"That went well dint-it?"* Now I was lost for words and during the journey home, Peter didn't stop recalling a catalogue of tales from his days in the projection room – typical!

1997 was the year that Hollywood gave us *Titanic* – which went down well – and I introduced Leiston to Professor Jingles and Robert Wolfe. I had known Brian Clarke (Professor Jingles) since my teenage days as a budding Punch and Judy man. Brian was, and still is, one of the UK's leading authorities on Punch and Judy, or 'Professors' as they are known – the showbiz title for Punch and Judy men. I used to travel around the holiday camps with Brian, helping him to set up, watching his show and then helping to pack it away – they were happy days. So, to get more bums on seats, I booked Brian to perform at the Film Theatre on a number of occasions. His appearances were a guaranteed success, providing that they were programmed in during the school holidays – you see, the way I have always seen it, the youngsters are tomorrow's audience and therefore, it is essential that they recognise the venue as a place of entertainment from an early age – that's why pantomime is so important to all theatres and besides all that, it's just nice to see families going to the cinema together – the excited children queuing up for their popcorn and then hearing them enjoying the film or show – it's pure magic that they cannot get from being huddled in front of a television screen.

I had first encountered the musical talents of Robert Wolfe as a teenager when, as part of a family holiday to Norfolk, I was taken along to The Thursford Collection – a collection of steam engines, mechanical organs, fairground rides and 'The Mighty Wurlitzer' show starring the man himself. I got in touch with his manager and that December, on a freezing cold night, Robert performed the first of many festive concerts to an appreciative packed house. That was also the night when Mr. Two Sticks fell over – we called him Mr. Two Sticks because he had two sticks!

The poor man was leaving the venue and as he was using the front steps, his two sticks slipped on the icy pavement, resulting in him crashing to the ground and bumping his head. Christina and I helped him up and back into the cinema, where we sat him down on a chair. I made a quick call to Dr. Simon Ball in Aldeburgh – these were the days when you could actually speak to your local doctor after hours – who was kind enough to come over and check that Mr. Two Sticks' injuries weren't serious and while we were waiting for the doctor to arrive, I asked Christina to fetch an ice lolly to place on the rising bump on his forehead, but when Christina returned with a Sparkle and gave it to him, he unwrapped it and started to suck it! We fetched another ice lolly and this time, placed it on his head.

We've had nick-names for many of our customers over the years – there was Old Grunter, who never spoke – he just threw his money on the counter and grunted. Then there was Mrs. Orgasm, who, if she enjoyed the film would provide a long, pleasurable sigh as she left the foyer – in fact, even if she didn't like the film, she would still groan as she left. Most recently, we have Mr. Credit-Watcher, who likes to watch all the credits at the end of each and every film –

where the film was made, who sang the song at the beginning and which company provided the catering!

Throughout much of 1998, the refurbishment of the Film Theatre continued, with thorough improvements made to the first floor area, to include the extension of the projection room, which involved the removal of the many sheets of the tin wall lining that remained from the days of nitrate film. Darren and I spent an entire day wrestling with layers of sharp tin, which had been in place since 1914 and took an awful of persuading to leave their fixings. We also took great delight in demolishing a partition wall that was separating the old rewind room and the director's room, to create a larger space that was destined to become my new office. Once the tin and dust had been removed, the ceilings were re-plastered, new flooring was fitted throughout and several coats of paint were applied to complete an incredible transformation in working conditions – from an absolute embarrassment to somewhere that was now a pleasant environment.

Hot on the heels of these latest works, Mr. Anthony Williams was invited to visit the Film Theatre and produce a comprehensive appraisal of the venues performance, its potential and a list of recommendations for the Town Council to consider. Anthony Williams had a vast experience in the international film and cinema industry and it was hoped that his visit to Leiston would inspire him to provide a list of recommendations to boost trade at the Film Theatre. He was a tiny man, in a well cut suit and sporting a neatly trimmed moustache – he was, as you would expect, very knowledgeable on all things cinema and highly inquisitive when it came to the operation of the venue and no cinema spool was left unturned during his inspection. Williams' paper was blunt and to the point – remarking that the council deserved praise for its support, which had enabled the local community to benefit from a cinema facility, during a long period of serious national decline for the cinema business and commenting that new cinemas had created expectations in comfort and film presentation among cinema audiences and that Leiston Film Theatre was currently at the stage where many independent cinemas were some 15 years earlier. The report made disappointing, but somehow predictable reading. He suggested various improvements to assist the Film Theatre – one of them was to turn it into a two or even three screen cinema, but this would have been far too costly. Top of his list was an upgrade in sound (something I had been droning on about for months), a facelift for the fascia and a suggestion of enlarging the foyer.

If any or all of Williams' suggestions were going to be completed, these were going to require mammoth expenditure and in consideration that Aldeburgh Cinema had previously received a £67,500 grant from the National Lottery for improvements to their foyer and auditorium in 1995, the Town Council thought that they too may be able attract such funding to assist in their own efforts to update the Film Theatre's interior. Councillor Frank Huxley and I travelled to Cambridge, where we were greeted by Antony Williams for a meeting with Eastern Arts to determine whether and how we might apply for a Lottery donation but on arrival and after a few short minutes, it seemed that criteria obstacles were being thrown in our path and it became very evident that the lid on the Lottery cash pot was proving difficult to open – possibly due to a certain Lottery project known as The Millennium Dome.

We were asked *"Would you ever consider commissioning a sculpture for your foyer as part of any grant application?"* I explained that our foyer was only 19ft long and 8ft wide and that there was hardly room for the customers to queue, without the addition of a sculpture. We were then told *"You may stand a better chance of success if you were to commission a work of art for the foyer, or perhaps introduce a gallery."* I replied that we'd rather have new seats! And so it went on and after an hour-or-so, it was summarised that, as the Film Theatre was owned by the Town Council, not a registered charity and that a neighbouring cinema had already been awarded a substantial sum of money, any application for Lottery grant aid would, in all probability, be unsuccessful. Frank and I drove back from Cambridge, gutted and muttering all the way – *"How did Aldeburgh Cinema get Lottery money when they're not a charity?"* I believed that the answer to that was quite simple – Lettie Gifford and their location.

111

The details of our visit were reported to the gathering of disappointed councillors, who were quite dismayed at the reception we had received in Cambridge. To date, the Town Council had invested £5,361 in Williams' advice and assistance and if they were willing to pursue a grant application – which we had been advised would, in all probability, be unsuccessful, an additional fee in the region of £9,740 would be payable for Williams to oversee our Lottery bid.

There appeared to be a distinct air of resilience at this particular meeting and it didn't take long for councillors to decide that, balanced against the unlikely Lottery payout, Williams' fee could be better spent on further improvements and suddenly, with council plumage suitably ruffled, the defiant members around the table were filling the room with compliments on what had already been achieved at the Film Theatre without Lottery support and having politely thanked Anthony Williams for all that he'd done, there was suddenly an unexpected enthusiasm to waste no more time and to proceed with the next phase of refurbishment as quickly as possible. All that was missing was an orchestra to burst into the Council Chamber with a rendition of *Land of Hope and Glory* and for the councillors to stand up and wave their Union Jack flags. Unbelievable!

It was hoped that another form of sponsorship and funding could be acquired elsewhere and the Support Club, who had been busy raising money and injecting financial support into the Film Theatre since 1992 were keen to do all they could to see this project completed and with Paul Snowden recently elected as the Support Club Chairman, the club were every bit as determined as the Town Council to see this project through.

Paul Snowden was one of Leiston's familiar characters that everyone of a certain age knew. He had worked at the Picture House throughout the 1960's and 70's as an usher – showing people to their seats and more infamously, banging them over the head with his torch and throwing them out if they made too much noise during the film. He was a good friend of Peter Free and was quite obviously passionate about the old Picture House. I say old, because as my 'relationship' with Paul developed, it was evident that he was one of those people who didn't embrace change easily – especially when it involved the Film Theatre. He was very vocal on certain issues and was furious at the thought of losing the auditorium murals and in a few months time would be firmly opposed to the new look auditorium – in fact I would go so far as saying that anything that altered the Picture House that he'd known and clearly loved was dismissed immediately. Over the years, Paul and I had numerous heated exchanges behind the scenes – some of which were, on occasions, an inferno of rants – we quite simply didn't get along. He is, however, fondly recalled by all those who were on the receiving end of his torch over the years!

In November 1999, Vivian Fox signed his contract of employment and became my second assistant manager – my first being Billy Lamb, who had worked as a projectionist (and a very good one too) at the Film Theatre for a number of years, before being offered the post as my assistant in March 1999, at a time when I was having to work ridiculous hours each week to stay on top of all that had to be done to maintain the expansion of our operation and oversee the continuing refurbishment works. Billy was a really good mate and we worked well together and would often go drinking to excess after work at The Black Horse – it helped that his mum was the landlady! When circumstances provoked Billy to leave almost overnight, it was decided that rather than employ from within, we would instead advertise the vacant position.

Vivian had been previously unsuccessful in being employed as a projectionist with us and had now returned, this time with the vacant office desk in his sights. There was no denying his enthusiasm for the town's cinema and his talents on a computer and so he became assistant number two, although it was evident that one day, he desired to sit in my chair.

" Leiston Film Theatre is fabulous.
I love going there as it's local and friendly.
We are very lucky to have a cinema so close
to home, with all the best films and, of course,
the brilliant pantomimes!
"

Keeping them in the picture

After all the excitement of the new Millennium, the year 2000 was going to be a dynamic 12 months, with new challenges at the Film Theatre. After many months of improvements almost everywhere else in the building it was finally time for refurbishment work to commence in the auditorium – and about time too. I only say this, because I was fully aware of the comprehensive improvements that had been made elsewhere in the building, but as far as the customers were concerned, they were still watching films in a cinema where the walls were decaying, the carpet was worn and some of the seats had more holes than a golf course! At least now, discussions could turn to a more suitable scheme of decoration for the auditorium and I had very firm ideas on how I wanted the finished product to look, but my 'vision' wasn't shared by everyone.

With a transformation just around the corner, I decided that it would be a good idea to stage another ladies night, before the auditorium received its make-over. We had made a good profit from the strip shows staged in the late 1990's and the popularity of the 1997 film *The Full Monty* had rekindled an appetite for these performances.

The show, entitled *The Big One* was one that we were producing ourselves – this time with a drag queen and three male strippers that were due to appear on stage in the May of 2000. Ticket sales had been fairly good and a few weeks before the strippers were due in town, a letter was received from the licensing department at Suffolk Coastal District Council, who were concerned at the content of this show and were reminding us that our license could be affected, if any part of the show were considered to be 'lewd or offensive' and this would include full frontal nudity. This proved to be a problem, as I knew only too well that the guys would definitely have their dangly bits out on our stage. If we proceeded with the show and a complaint was made, we would end up in hot water. If I made the performers keep their pants on, I would have a high heeled riot on my hands. If we cancelled the show, we would be safe and what's more, we could gain a lot of publicity from this. It didn't take a lot of thinking through and within the hour a press release had been penned and was faxed to all local newspapers and radio. The following day, I opened the East Anglian Daily Times to see that the story was domineering the whole of page 5, with the headline *"Full Monty: You can see it on screen but not in the flesh"* It was brilliant publicity – complete with bemused comments from the outraged townsfolk and a comment from the Assistant Chief Executive at Suffolk Coastal District Council. The story also made the BBC Radio Suffolk breakfast programme and the hourly news bulletins throughout the day – a marvellous result.

Despite all the excellent media coverage, which had helped to raise the awareness of the venue, I had been thoroughly annoyed at having to cancel this show and was more than a little interested to learn, only a few weeks later, that *The Ultimate Fantasy Show* was due to appear at The Spa Pavilion Theatre in Felixstowe five months later – the very show that had thrilled the ladies of Leiston back in 1995. I was well aware of the level of 'exposure' that this show featured and was thrilled to know that full frontal nudity would be almost certainly be appearing at a theatre, which was owned by Suffolk Coastal District Council.

A plan was hatched. Firstly, I would write to Suffolk Coastal, asking them to confirm that the performance at the Spa Pavilion would not contain full frontal nudity. You may imagine my delight, when a prompt reply was received, confirming that the show would not contain such nudity. Next, two tickets were purchased for a couple of female spies to infiltrate the front row and to obtain photographic evidence of the meat-and-two-veg – and I didn't mean their pre-show pub meal!

And so, on a chilly October night, two eager women enjoyed the

'Ultimate Girls Night Out', snapping away with their cameras, whenever a trouser snake appeared! The photographs provided all the proof that I needed and another press release was issued, this time grabbing us another full page spread on page 3, with the headline *"This is naked hypocrisy!"* The article was a masterpiece – with promoters and theatre bosses adamant that there had been no full frontal nudity and me, with photos in hand, using phrases such as *"They've been caught with their trousers down!"* The story had yet again provided us with a huge amount of publicity and from what I was told, made me very unpopular for a while at Suffolk Coastal's offices.

Right, back to the auditorium redecoration. I was adamant that the auditorium walls should be draped with suitable material, from the ceiling to a pelmet, with the lower half of the auditorium walls, boarded over with plasterboard and then covered with carpet. I was extremely passionate about this and knew that this was not only a cost effective solution in redecorating the vast area of the auditorium walls, it would also totally transform the appearance – it seriously needed to shake off that 'flea-pit' image – it needed a new identity.

The council were happy to fund the cost of the drapes and the Support Club had pledged to pay for the wood, plasterboard and skirting board, so that improvements could be made almost immediately. Money was clearly tight and if the auditorium walls were going to ever get done, we were going to have to do as much as we could ourselves – so that's exactly what we did – and before anyone could change their mind! Vivian and I constructed the pelmet that the drapes would tuck into – we were no carpenters, but we seemed to do a pretty good job. Next, we fixed sheets and sheets of plasterboard to the lower section of the auditorium walls, which would eventually be covered with carpet to provide a more sumptuous appearance and be beneficial to the cinema acoustics. Finally, new skirting board was fitted to the bottom of the plasterboard, before all holes were filled and the pelmet and skirting board was painted in a colour that I jokingly named 'Palladium Red' – that is of course, utter trash – it's really a colour from the

Dulux paint range, but it seemed to be embraced by the council and the public and so we've gone along with it ever since. This all sounds very easy and quick, but these works were being conducted alongside our daily duties and took a good few weeks to complete – but at least our customers could see that something was happening and they genuinely seemed quite excited at the prospect of gaining a 'new-look' cinema.

So far, the refurbished auditorium hadn't cost the council much at all. The drapes had cost £2,450, the Support Club had purchased all the other materials, including the carpeting fitted to the bottom half of the side walls and Vivian and I had done all the labour. It all seemed to be going so well – so well in fact, that we were almost waiting for something to go wrong and when it did, it almost closed the venue down. On an inspection of the refurbishment work, the Fire Service, who were, by the way, very impressed with our efforts, had objected to carpeting being fitted to the walls – not the fabric itself, as that was flame retardant. The objection was due to the foam rubber backing and the fact that, should this ignite, fire could easily spread, obviously putting lives at risk. The wheels of progress came to a grinding halt and we were very firmly instructed not to put the heating on (not ideal in the winter months) and were given two weeks to find an alternative wall covering, or we would have to remove the carpeting from the walls – although we were quite welcome to retain it and use it on the floor!

A frantic few days followed – letters were written, faxes were sent and I received a right royal kick up the arse from the Town Council! But what really bothered me, was the fact that the Support Club had paid for the carpeting, which now had to be removed – which it was a few days later, with no replacement wall covering, that conformed to the necessary safety standard in sight.

This meant that the first Film Theatre pantomime in eight years was going to be presented with the walls half completed. The pantomime in question was Goldilocks and the Three Bears – a jointly produced production between the Film Theatre and the Bright Sparks amateur dramatics group, who hadn't performed at the venue since 1993. The group was initiated by Joan Girling (there she is again) and a few of the ladies from the Leiston Women's Institute, who had outgrown the W.I. hut and felt that they wanted to put on a show in their local theatre – they surmised that their efforts would either be a 'damp squib' or a 'bright spark' and that's where the name came from. I had written to the group in the spring of 2000, asking them if they would be prepared to return to the Film Theatre to stage a jointly produced pantomime in the January of 2001 – this was always considered to be the best time for these shows, as they were always looked upon as a post Christmas treat – plus we'd sell lots of tickets as Christmas gifts! The group accepted my invitation and a thirteen year working relationship was born – well, thirteen and counting at the time of writing this book!

It was at this point that I encountered Stephen Ginger. His great grandfather Ted Titlow had been one of the original shareholders in the Picture House and his uncle Colin has been a Town Councillor since 1987. Stephen and I share a common trait – we are perfectionists and prefer to do things properly and this made a good base for this pantomime to build on. The Film Theatre would fund the production costs, I would act as the director for the show and everything else would be jointly produced by the venue and the group – this included the writing of the script, the building of sets and the making of costumes.

A small team would meet once a week to write the script – complete with numerous scripted digs at certain local residents and businesses and as soon as this was completed, parts would be allocated to the amateur cast, consisting of builders, painters and supermarket supervisors. Costumes were made, props were prepared and a set was built – we needed Goldilocks' house, a wood, the Three Bears house – complete with three chairs and beds and not forgetting a circus tent – the villainess ringmaster wanted to trap the bears and make them the main attraction (boo)! Nobody imagined the amount of work that was involved in putting this show together and as three months of rehearsals came to an end and the opening night crept ever nearer, there was still an awful lot left to do – so much so that when that initial performance arrived, the stage crew was warned to be careful when moving the Three Bears house, as the paint on the set was still wet!

After the many months of dedicated work, the four sell-out performances were a complete and utter success, rewarding the cast with well deserved plaudits across the community. However, after reflecting on the sheer level of work involved in creating the show, the exhausted group decided that their pantomimes would have to be a bi-annual event and in the following years further jointly produced productions including Cinderella (2003), Red Riding Hood (2005) and Aladdin (2007) – this was the one when I ashamedly lost my rag during the dress rehearsal and stormed out of the venue shouting obscenities as I went – not a moment that I'm particularly proud of, but one that Stephen remembers well. As the rehearsal came to an abrupt pause, Stephen attempted to calm me down while trying to contain his laughter, as I continued ranting upstairs – dressed as Widow Twanky! A short while later I returned to the stage, apologised, the rehearsal continued and the pantomime was another huge triumph.

By 2009, the pantomimes were playing to 1,200 eager panto-goers over five performances with Snow White and the Seven Dwarfs becoming the fastest selling one of all – so much so, that one of the dress rehearsals was opened up as an additional performance to meet demand. This was also the pantomime where we first utilised the talents of Suffolk musician Tom Horton. I had known Tom since the age of 14, when he was a contestant in one of our talent shows. Tom's natural flair as a musician made an immediate impact on the 'slickness' of our pantomimes – by introducing live music to these productions and more importantly, being able to introduce little things such as a drum and a symbol crash when a dame falls flat on her backside, or a gentle underscore during scene changes – it makes a vast difference to the production values and makes the performances even more polished. We've used Tom, now aged 31, in all of our pantomimes ever since – Treasure Island (2010), Jack and the Beanstalk (2012) and Cinderella (2013) and he remains the most expensive part of our pantomime process, whose fee is thankfully offset by the generosity of various sponsors.

As the years have progressed, so has our production process. We no longer make any of the sets, preferring to hire all the scenery and most of the costumes are items featured in the Film Theatre's extensive costume hire collection. Please don't go thinking that these pantomimes are any easier to stage – they still require a considerable amount of dedication and commitment from all those involved to produce what is, nowadays, an annual affair and one of the highlights in the Film Theatre calendar – the last pantomime played to an audience of 2,100 over seven separate performances – oh yes it did!

Our upcoming centenary pantomime is The Wonderful Wizard of Oz: The Pantomime, in which I'm playing the roles of Professor Marvel and the Wizard himself. I always wanted to bring this story to the pantomime stage and our 100th anniversary has provided the excuse I needed to tackle such an ambitious production. In our version, Professor Marvel is a travelling showman, touring the land to spread the word about a Picture Palace that's 100 years old – fancy that!

Back in the February of 2001, with the bottom half of the auditorium walls still bare plasterboard, I was starting to worry. Then, with the help of a firm in Beccles, we located a suitable wall covering that had to be imported, but thankfully conformed to the relevant fire safety standards. The material was ordered and within a few days of arrival, a working party was assembled to install the new wall covering. There was a huge sigh of relief when, finally, the auditorium walls were completed, although I did wonder if this experience may provoke the Town Council to call a halt to plans to continue with the critical phase of the entire refurbishment, but it seemed that the transformation (and the voluntary efforts of their staff) in the auditorium had reignited the council's desire to see this project completed.

A grant from Suffolk Coastal District Council, a contribution from the Town Council and the funds raised from a 'sponsor-a-seat' campaign had produced significant finances to enable the refurbishment of the auditorium seating, re-decorate that filthy ceiling and provide new carpeting throughout – this time with underlay as the old one had been glued directly to the floorboards, resulting in loud thuds from youngsters feet when they ran to the toilets – especially that loose floorboard in the centre aisle that rattled whenever a child ran over it! In keeping with the previous and thorough refurbishment phases, the Town Council engaged the services of Frank Bilton once again, to ensure that the floor was sound throughout before any work commenced, especially after a flood in 1993 when Leiston had been subjected to a torrential downpour overnight and I came into work to discover that the auditorium was half under water – it really was – right up to the centre aisle. The rainfall had been so overwhelming that the drains couldn't cope and the filthy water had found its way under the side exit doors. Although Bilton's report concluded that it was entirely safe, it was considered prudent to treat the timbers as a matter of course – the once neglected Film Theatre was now receiving the ultimate care in doing the job well and I liked this approach.

I had been asked to draw up a schedule of works – a timescale to run by and a ground plan of any potential new layouts – and to make sure that any materials used were entirely flame retardant! I can still recall the smug phrase *"We've already had our fingers burnt once!"* being used. Much consideration was given to the seating design of the new auditorium – whether to go with all new chairs or refurbish the existing traditional tip-up seats. It really wasn't a big consideration – we were proudly boasting to be Suffolk's oldest cinema, so it seemed obvious that we should retain the characteristic charm of the traditional seating. We made contact with a number of firms, many of which wanted to flog us their new state-of-the-art plastic chairs – probably because they didn't like the idea of all the work that came with refurbishing 300 seats. It was Liz and Rob from Sussex Seating, who immediately 'clicked' with me and understood my objectives and instead of trying to discourage us, they actually worked with us, in creating a number of seating layouts to consider.

In 2000, the auditorium had two blocks of seating, with a large aisle at the front and in the centre, separating the two blocks. There were

16/17 seats to a row and this made things difficult when somebody need to visit the toilet during a film or show, as they would have to disturb everyone around them as they stood up and moved along the row, muttering a succession of *"Scuse me, thank you ... Scuse me, thank you!"* and then there was the inevitable return *"Scuse me, thank you ... Scuse me, thank you!"*. I had five key objectives in designing any proposed new seating layout - to introduce a four block seating plan, reduce the size of the current aisle width, increase the number of wheelchair spaces for disabled customers, boost the amount of legroom between the rows and increase the seating capacity in the process from 292 to 304 (including three wheelchair spaces). This was quite a big ask, but Liz and Rob came up with a plan, which would tick all my boxes, but this was not a popular option for the Town Council, who were concerned that the seats were to be located in uniformed rows and not staggered – it was noted that *"shorter members were concerned that this would hinder their view"*. This was an initial concern of mine too, but Liz and Rob satisfied these worries. The nervous council arranged a site meeting with the Fire Service and Licensing Authority to confirm that the materials to be used conformed to British Safety Standards and that the proposed aisle width met with the current regulations and once these issues were clarified, the new seating layout was carried at the vote and work could now commence in planning when exactly to carry out this major improvement.

Refurbishing cinema seats is a little like shopping in a supermarket – you have your value range and you have your premium brand. I wanted the auditorium seating to boast the best in comfort and legroom that we could afford and it was ultimately decided that we would use the cold cure foam – Liz told me that the heat from your body shapes the foam to the contours of your bum! I also insisted on using 100% wool fabric, as this was hard wearing and Liz told me that they use this material on British Railways, so I knew we were on the right track! To complete the look of the new seats, Rob suggested that we covered the back of the seats with matching fabric, rather than just painting the wood and that the grubby cast iron metalwork was sprayed in a traditional gold colour – my thoughts exactly.

I was determined to manage this phase myself, to ensure that everything was executed exactly how I wanted it to be and because I still had the bruising from my council beating over the wall covering! So, taking the many aspects of the works into account, I concluded that a three-week closure would be necessary to re-vamp the auditorium and on top of all this, I decided that we'd refurbish the foyer at the same time! The plan sounds quite easy and went like this – firstly, the seats were all removed and transported to Chichester for refurbishment. Next, the raised platforms for the rear seats would be removed (the hardest days work I have ever endured – they really didn't mean these to ever come up!). While the foyer was prepared for redecoration, the painters would have three days to paint the ceiling (twice) and then a party of volunteers would take up the horrible old yellow cord carpet (remember, this had been stuck down using industrial adhesive). We would then continue painting in the foyer, while the carpet firm arrived to board where the new seating would be, but the hardboard had to be removed the following morning, when the cold temperatures had caused the boarding to curl up - replacing it with plywood was the only option. Next the lino was laid to the plywood panels and industrial underlay and carpet was fitted to the foyer, lobby and auditorium aisle. Finally, after many splinters, sweaty tee-shirts and bursts of occasional foul language, the day arrived for the 301 plush red seats to be installed.

Rob and his team arrived, had a coffee, checked the measurements of the seating area, which were of course spot on and then, with much anticipation, the refurbished seats were stacked to one side of the auditorium, ready for fitting the following day – and they really did look very, very nice. The auditorium was already looking absolutely amazing and you cannot imagine how excited I was at the prospect of what was about to happen during the following day – in fact, I hardly slept that night and was down the cinema by 7am with my tail firmly wagging!

Chalk lines were located to the auditorium floor, all allowing for precisely the same amount of generous leg room. Then, starting at the back, rows of seating were slowly fixed into place and by lunchtime, we were almost half way. It was a glorious day and the sun was beaming into the auditorium through the open exit doors, with the dust depicting the sunlight a little like smoke in a spotlight. We were all on our knees fixing down the rows of new seating when a silhouette appeared at one the side doors – it was Peter Free. There was a genuine feeling of pleasure from those present when we realised who it was. *"This all looks very nice. Good luck to you."* said Peter and by the time I'd got to my feet to invite him in for a cuppa, he'd gone. I went to the exit door, but there was no sign of Peter anywhere. That was the last time that he ever came to the Film Theatre, despite inviting him to the official opening of the new auditorium a few days later.

The auditorium project had been completed with only a day to spare and the Film Theatre re-opened, as promised, on Friday 20th July 2001 with the film *Shrek*. I was overwhelmed by what we had achieved. We had worked 14-16 hour days to get to this stage and it had definitely been worth all the sheer hard work. I couldn't wait to get on the telephone and invite Suffolk's media to come and share in our success. We gained the all important column centimetres in the local press and had the obligatory Town Council viewing, but the most rewarding part for me was the wonderful comments received from our customers – old and new, who were greatly impressed with the cinema's re-vamped surroundings, especially the comfortable 'new' seats. As I saw it, the future of the Film Theatre was looking a lot brighter, but I still had more plans up my sleeve – it was just a question of letting the dust settle before I hit the council with my next bright idea.

The new look auditorium provided the venue with a bumper summer season of curious customers, with films like *Cats and Dogs* proving very popular. It was during this particular films run that projectionist David Ward kindly answered the box office telephone one busy afternoon. *"Hullo, Leiston Film Theatre"* said David, to which the lady caller enquired *"Can you tell me what's showing at the moment?"* *"Cats and Dorgs"* replied David, in his dry Suffolk accent. *"Cats and what?"* asked the lady. *"Cats and Dorgs"* said David (giggling). *"And who's in that?"* she asked. *"A load of old cats and a load of old dorgs!"* laughed David. The lady did actually bring her family to see the film that tea-time and seeing the funny side of her telephone experience, asked for tickets to see *Cats and Dorgs*! David Ward came to work at the Film Theatre after recovering from serious illness. He was a terrific guy, with a dry sense of humour and an infectious chuckle and we shared many, many laughs in his company – like the day he and Brian Ginger volunteered to paint the front of the stage during the auditorium refurbishment. Brian started on one side, with David on the other and it wasn't until they met in the centre that they realised that one had been using gloss paint and the other had been using matt emulsion! He was a very conscientious projectionist and took great pride in putting on a great show – he was one of the best. David left our employment in 2002, to pursue his ambition of running his own angling shop in Saxmundham and very sadly passed away in 2013. Belinda and I attended his funeral at a packed church and I was especially touched to hear how much he enjoyed his time spent at the Film Theatre (and our banter) during his eulogy.

As the positive reviews of our new-look auditorium spread around the locality and the various film distributors were advised of our achievements, we were offered the opportunity to screen a little film by the name of *Harry Potter and the Philosophers Stone* from its UK release date in November 2001. Warner Bros. had acquired the rights to the Harry Potter books in 1999 and there was no doubt that these films had the potential to be cinematic gold – or at least bring a shed load of customers through the box office – and they did! Customers queued along Leiston High Street for two weeks solid to enjoy the first film – breaking all our existing box office records in the process and over the following 10 years, the Film Theatre was the only independent cinema locally to screen all seven films from their relevant release dates (the final instalment – *Harry Potter and the Deathly Hallows* being released in two parts in 2010 and 2011). Quite an achievement for a small rural cinema. We were even graced with the presence of a young Ed Sheeran, who visited us to enjoy a midnight screening of the *Deathly Hallows Pt 2* – much to the excitement of the teenage girls in the auditorium.

This was also the year when a certain yellow bear and his squeaky best friend would make their debut appearance at the Film Theatre. I refer of course to Sooty and Sweep, who caused much excitement in the town when they took to our stage in October 2001. This was a big deal for us – The Sooty Show was a large touring show, used to filling the larger venues around the country and to have the quietest puppet in show-business paying us a visit was a childhood dream come true for me. You see, as a youngster, my brother Graham and sister-in-law Sue, would take me on holiday with them (to give my mum and dad a break no doubt) and it was while I was on one of these holidays that I crazed for a set of Sooty and Sweep puppets. Having proved that pester power prevails, I'm told that I spent the rest of the holiday entertaining crowds of children, who were sitting on the grass, with me wiggling Sooty and Sweep from the open car window!

Anyway, back to the Film Theatre and to make Sooty pay, we embarked on probably the biggest awareness campaign we had ever created; with Hit Entertainment (the new owners of Sooty after Matthew Corbett had sold up) sending the new Sooty presenter Richard Cadell down to do the necessary radio and newspaper interviews and the obligatory water pistol photo outside the Film Theatre. They even sent a set of giant mascot style Sooty and Sweep costumes, which we placed into the Aldeburgh carnival procession to promote the fact that Sooty was coming to town – poor Katie Hegarty (Sooty) and Maria Stickland (Sweep) had to endure over two hours in those stifling costumes, in scorching weather conditions and when the sweaty pair were finally unzipped, they looked as if they had swam the channel!

The day of the show arrived, with two separate sell-out performances ahead of us and with a little bit of give and take, the set finally squeezed onto our stage – you see, the set – a hotel – had been designed for the larger venue stages and ours was considerably smaller. Richard arrived and after a brief rehearsal and sound check (I was doing the sound), all was ready to go and once the hoards of excited children had purchased their Sooty souvenirs and taken their seats, it was time for the fun to begin – and oh how they laughed – custard pies, silly jokes and Sweep performing Pavarotti – the kids loved it and to be totally honest, so did we!

All was going very well until Richard was leaving the stage to fetch something for Sooty and as he did, there was a thud and we noticed that the entire set wobbled. The show suddenly fell silent – with Sooty, Sweep and Sue left stranded on stage and after 30-or-so seconds had passed, Richard returned and delivered his next line. Stephen (on the lights) and I looked at each other and judging by the obvious gash on Richard's forehead, we knew that something had gone horribly wrong. Because they had adjusted the set to fit our stage, Richard had caught his head on a piece of scenery that wouldn't normally have been there, which as a result had produced a large cut, which was bleeding quite heavily. A few more seconds went by and a pale Richard was forced to leave the stage, leaving the puppets behind and as all the characters voices were on disc, even the puppeteers couldn't help. After a further minute Richard reappeared, this time with a white towel wrapped around his head and as he explained what had happened to the audience, the blood was seeping through the towel.

Having almost reached the interval, Richard persevered through, like a true professional, to the end of the first half and as the interval came and ice creams were sold, there were frantic goings on backstage to calm Richard's bleeding and to decide whether to continue with the show. I didn't want the show to be cancelled, as we'd worked so hard in filling the venue full of youngsters who were thoroughly enjoying themselves. On the other hand, I didn't relish the idea of a Sooty TV presenter bleeding to death on our stage. I needn't have worried though, as Richard was adamant that he would continue with the performances – and he did – much to the appreciation of the audience – he even stayed behind to say hello (with Sooty of course) to the winner of a schools colouring competition we had organised to promote the show. He was a damn nice chap. Sooty came and went and the children spoke about him for months afterwards and we knew that we simply had to invite

Sooty back again in the following year, which we did – with a set that had this time been designed to fit our stage! However on this occasion, his appearance resulted in Sweep's bath time antics creating a major fuss and a war of words between our insurance companies.

In the August of 2002, our lavish new velvet stage curtains were installed, thanks to a donation from the Film Theatre Support Club and match funding which came via a grant from – yes, you guessed it, County Councillor Joan Girling! The new curtains really added that finishing touch to our new look auditorium and before anyone asks, they were fully flame retardant and had been treated with a specialist chemical to make them stage proof – something that Sooty and friends hadn't considered when they decided to give a protesting Sweep a bath at the end of the first half during their second visit to the Film Theatre. We were told that the curtains were to close with Sweep still in the bath and so, after a song and a link into the interval, the curtains were closed and as they did, the foam being used for the bath scene accidently came into contact with the material and reacted with the flame retardant treatment, causing large discoloured circles to appear on our brand new curtains. I was bloody furious and a few days later, a claim was made against Sooty for replacement curtains. What followed was a bitter exchange of letters from one insurer to another and before you could say *Izzy wizzy let's get busy*, an identical pair of curtains appeared and Sooty became the first and only puppet ever to be banned from the Film Theatre – although technically, it was entirely Sweeps fault!

Around this time, I'd been spending a number of years performing my comedy cabaret act in most of the region's top holiday centres – Pontins, Haven and the like, plus a stint for the prestigious Thomson Gold resorts. During my travels I'd made extensive contacts with many fellow artistes and throughout the late nineties and early 'noughties' I brought many of these various acts to appear at the Film Theatre in numerous variety shows that I was producing for the venue – one of which was to celebrate the venue's 90th anniversary in 2004. We also played host to a number of more familiar names – Patrick Moore (with his xylophone), Ireland's Mary Duff, Joe Brown and the Bruvvers, Chas 'n' Dave, Jimmy Cricket and not forgetting Zippy, George and Bungle from Rainbow – the real Zippy, George and Bungle, unlike The Spiceish Girls – an awful tribute act to The Spice Girls – five little wannabes who offered the impression that they were the real thing – pretentious little divas!

That's one thing I've never entertained from any artiste appearing at the Film Theatre – an ego. If they have their head up their arse, they never return to our stage again. I found Patrick Moore to be quite rude – he insisted that I call him 'Sir. Patrick'. Mary Duff was (and still is) quite lovely and has appeared on our stage many times as a result, although I was quite alarmed when I first met her and she asked me *"Where do you go for the crack in Leiston?"* At first, I thought she meant drugs, until somebody explained that by 'crack' (correctly spelt craic) she was actually referring to 'a good time' – for one moment I thought I had another scoop for the East Anglian Daily Times! I'd been warned that Joe Brown could be a temperamental so-and-so, but I found him to be a total gent and an incredible musician and he was very complimentary about the Film Theatre. Bringing comedy legend Jimmy Cricket to town was a real coup too – I'd worked with Jimmy during a Children in Need variety show, that I had produced for BBC Radio Suffolk in 2005 and meeting this man, who I had laughed at on television and stage during my childhood, was a genuine thrill and he was such a lovely guy that I knew we had to book him to appear at our venue.

I was quite excited about meeting Chas 'n' Dave too. As with most live shows, the 'crew' usually arrive during the afternoon to prepare the stage, rig the sound equipment and basically load everything into the venue. Then, around tea-time, the artistes will arrive and proceed to set up their instruments. When Joe Brown appeared at the Film Theatre, he conducted the most comprehensive sound check I've ever witnessed prior to a show – over an hour to make sure that everything was perfect. With Chas 'n' Dave, things were quite different.

Their sound *'Geezer'* (let's call him Steve) had arrived after lunch and installed the relevant cables, speakers and sound desk ready for the arrival of the famous cockney duo. By 6pm, I was starting to worry as there wasn't any sign of Chas 'n' Dave, but Steve assured me that they would be arriving in plenty of *'Lager and Lime'* (time). Soon it was 6.30pm and I was now entering panic mode, with the knowledge that hundreds of theatre-goers would be packing into the *'Stevie Nicks'* (flicks) in half an hour expecting a bit of *Rabbit Rabbit Rabbit* at 7.30pm. At 6.45pm there was a bang on the side door. I opened it and in walked Chas, followed by Dave, followed by their drummer (the one who always wore a trilby). They placed their instruments on the stage and Chas asked *"Where's the nearest pub?"* *"The Black Horse at the traffic lights"* I replied. *"What time are we on?"* asks Dave. *"7.30"* I said. *"Meet us round the back just before"* said Chas and with that, he and Dave – and the one with the trilby sped up the side passage and on to the pub. It was Steve who then set up the instruments and proceeded to run through a sound check on his *'Jack Jones'* (alone).

At 7.25pm, I was pacing up and down the *'Apples and Pears'* (stairs) in the backstage corridor when there was knock on the dressing room door. It was Chas, Dave and – well, you know the gag by now! They had a quick *'Jimmy Riddle'* (piddle) and went straight on stage to perform an excellent first half of 'unplugged' skiffle music. It really was a very enjoyable 45 minutes and as the appreciative audience tucked into their ice creams during the interval, the musical trio returned to the *'German Cruiser'* (boozer) to enjoy another bevy or two.

All seemed to be going well and with the Support Club raffle (a vital part of any live show at the Film Theatre) out of the way, Chas 'n' Dave took to the stage, this time very much 'plugged' to perform all their greatest hits – very noisy hits. The volume in the auditorium was so great that the show could be heard in the neighbouring streets. In fact, it was so ridiculously loud that a number of the audience were sitting with their fingers in their ears and some were soon on their feet and heading for the foyer where, above the noise vibrating from the stage, were complaining about the rowdy performance. I went and Steve and eventually managed to convey our opinion sound was far too loud – and his reply? *"Nothin' I can do about mate"*. Was he kidding? He had umpteen buttons in front of him and was unable to reduce the volume? By the time Chas 'n' Dave got to perform *Ain't no pleasing you*, many of the audience had left their seats and the venue. Even I had a headache.

I wrote an abrupt letter to their management the following day advising them that, as a result of their deafening performance, we wouldn't be looking to invite Chas 'n' Dave back to the Film Theatre, which was a genuine shame. If an actual sound check had been attempted and volume levels considered, it would have been an excellent night of entertainment. I never did receive a reply.

Turning a corner

At the Leiston Town Council Annual General Meeting in May 2003, the Chairman, Michael Taylor, commented that *"Over the past 12 years, the Film Theatre has become an asset to Leiston."* Yes it had. The building had been completely refurbished from top to bottom, with no corners being cut to create a brilliant venue that the town really could be proud of and one that now offered everything that the big city cinemas did. It was also the year that David Gooderham retired as Town Clerk, to be replaced by John Rayner. I had been working alongside David for 11 years, carefully developing the Film Theatre into the venue it had become and I was more than a little nervous at the appointment of a new clerk – what if he couldn't care less whether the cinema remained open or closed – or what if we didn't see eye-to-eye? Thankfully, John was enthusiastic about having a cinema in the town and had been well and truly educated on the journey that David and I had endured to get to this point and so I was quietly confident that John and I would get along – and we did – and still do! He is an excellent officer of the town, with the patience of a saint and although we share a professional association, we have the kind of working relationship that allows us to be frank and honest with each other. There have been times when I've gone absolutely nuts in the office over something-or-other and then there's occasions when I'm overjoyed and whatever my mood, he listens and offers advice, encouragement and praise where necessary. He's a good guy and I feel fortunate to work with somebody like him.

2003 also saw the Film Theatre Support Club embark on their grandest scheme to date. It was proposed that the club would fund the replacement of the ancient lighting equipment, to include new dimmer racks, stage lights, scenery tracking, as well as sets of new stage curtains and automated tracking for the masking and curtains – remember, we were still winding the curtains by hand from the projection room! This was going to be a massive undertaking for the club, who in the coming months threw themselves into raising the funds to make this plan a reality. Coffee mornings, sausage sizzles, quiz nights and all manner of events were organised to raise the funds necessary to bring this project to fruition. The club also received several generous grants totalling £12,210, which really helped things move along.

The Town Council continued to make their own improvements – a new external clock, to replace the rusted one removed during the 1994 refurbishment and another coat of paint for the front exterior.

You may recall that in 1998 the Town Council had engaged the services of Anthony Williams to produce a report on the venues performance and potential. As a result of Williams' report, my own recommendations and personal observations of the council (that the existing sound was terrible), it was ultimately decided that the venue should upgrade to Dolby digital sound - the current Dolby sound processor was now 16 years old and had actually gone out of production around the time of its installation! You simply couldn't obtain spare parts if you needed to, so there really was little alternative. I was very pleased to be made responsible for obtaining the quotes for the installation of a Dolby digital sound processor and quickly made contact with two of the industry's prominent suppliers. One of the visiting engineers was Steve Grant – the same Steve Grant who was party to the April fool's day joke at Aldeburgh Cinema some 16 years earlier! Having this 'relationship' with Steve made this process easy and my brief to Steve was quite simple – I wanted the best sound system that we could afford. Steve ensured that the advice and equipment that was offered for installation was exactly that, from the digital sound processor and new speakers, to the wires and plugs. I was entirely confident that the proposed equipment was going to be top-notch kit and dare I say, a 'sound' investment! Having previously encountered Steve, I knew that we could look forward to a first class installation and by installing the new equipment in May, Steve would avoid another practical joke! The new Dolby Digital Surround EX sound system was finally installed in the May of 2007 and showcased with the release of *Pirates of the Caribbean: At Worlds End.*

In February 2008, Paul Snowden stood down as Chairman of the Film Theatre Support Club after 15 years service, during which time many major improvements had been made at the cinema, including their ambitious 'Set the Stage' project, which had taken five years to complete, at a total cost of £33,000 – an amazing achievement. Paul was succeeded by Lesley Hill as the new Chairman, who immediately brought her 'no-nonsense' approach to the committee meetings and soon had the band of volunteers busily raising more funds for my next grand plan. Lesley has now been the Support Club Chairman for five years and links between the club and Film Theatre management have never been stronger – she is a very assertive officer for the organisation and whole heartedly supports most things that we do at the Film Theatre.

Next on the Williams hit list was a new fascia at the Film Theatre and in his appraisal, he had hinted that a protruding canopy style fascia might be more modern looking and detract from the 'old' image, with floodlighting to highlight the prominence of the building. However, the powers that be were not convinced with the idea of an extended fascia and neither was I – it would have been quite unsightly on the High Street and in my opinion, a complete waste of money. It was January 2008 before this matter was eventually brought to the council table and when it was, the canopy notion was dismissed entirely. A slatted wooden fascia had been fitted to the front exterior in 1985 and through neglected maintenance was now in a very poor condition – faded and worn, with some panels missing – not a good advertisement for the state-of-the-art cinema inside.

The council recognised that a new fascia was required as *a good advertisement,* to *enhance the town* and *be a one-off cost with no ongoing repairs to the current fascia.* So, with this in mind, the following months were spent considering various options for updating the Film Theatre entrance. Some remarked that the present wooden frontage was part of the building and integral to the image of being the oldest cinema in Suffolk. Others felt that a more modern appearance would be more appropriate. As you might expect, I had strong views on this and was adamant that we should give the fascia a new look – vibrant, inviting, theatrical and most importantly, gold lettering spelling LEISTON FILM THEATRE and not just FILM THEATRE as was preferred in 1985.

The debate continued and at their meeting in May 2008, council members decided that they would prefer to remove the current wooden fascia and replace it with an identical wooden fascia on a 'like-for-like' basis, but with subtle lighting to illuminate the building at night. I couldn't believe what I was hearing and as the July meeting approached, I was doing everything I could to make councillors see sense that this absolutely wasn't, in my opinion, the best option. Thankfully, the quotations received for a new wooden fascia appeared to be more costly than anyone had first imagined and so, hasty repairs were made to make the present signage safe ahead of the summer season and a final decision was postponed until a later date – a much later date, possibly due to the distraction of Williams' third and final vision for an improved Film Theatre.

In April 2008, I placed a controversial proposal before the council that they should consider taking back one of their shops and convert it into an enlarged foyer and provide a combined area for box office and refreshments – something that had been mentioned on umpteen occasions over the years, but one that nobody had actually had the conviction to explore further.

If successful, this would mean that the council would have to serve notice to the Bertie's Barber Shop that they intended to terminate the lease – something that I knew would be an uncomfortable experience. Jan Pickett (the barber) had taken on the lease of the shop in August 1992 and had built up what appeared to be a thriving business, with me being one of her loyal customers. Jan and I had always got along well, mainly due to her direct manner – she always spoke her mind – and still does! Bertie's was also infamous for its 'humorous' chalked messages on the board outside including 'HAVE IT OFF HERE' and POP IN FOR THE SNIP.'

I was asked to prepare a business plan for the scheme, to be presented to the full council when completed and so, the following six months was spent preparing a detailed 16 page report that covered everything from the proposal itself and its objectives, to floor plans and even a case study on the Little Theatre in Sheringham, which had embarked on something similar at their venue, resulting in a significant financial improvement to their income. My plan also included information on the timescale of the works, various potential savings and additional income, the project expenditure, funding and a statement that this proposal was my personal vision for the future development of the Film Theatre, in an attempt to make it somewhat financially viable – or at least reduce that deficit. I was certainly never on any mission to cause Jan any grief – the way I saw it, I was simply doing what I was employed to do – what I considered to be best for the venue.

With the unanimous support of the Film Theatre Support Club committee, and Jan's 948 signature petition and claims that my proposals would increase the council's financial 'burden' on the town, the arguments for and against continued over the following months.

One of the main objectives of my proposal was to provide proper access for our elderly and disabled customers, or indeed anyone who was unable to negotiate the front steps. Up until now, the only access for these patrons was via the bottom side exit door – hardly ideal on a cold or wet day. I had enrolled the assistance of one of our regular customers, who had to wait outside, in whatever the weather, for his partner to queue up for tickets and notify the staff that he was waiting at the side door to be let in and vice-versa at the end of the film.

It was also paramount that, if this project was given the green light to proceed, then the works would be at no cost to the council – not one single penny. The Support Club were 100% behind me and had indicated that they would pick up the bill for any materials. I had called upon the generosity of several friends and local businesses –

137

we even received a couple of anonymous donations from members of the public to help fund the project.

I was very proud of my report. I had devoted a great deal of time and effort into creating what I considered to be a thorough study. As far as I was concerned, all the evidence in favour of my proposal was contained within the report and providing that it had been read in full, a business mind would have clearly identified the opportunity presented. The papers were presented to all councillors in September 2008 and tabled for discussion at their November meeting. The Town Council meeting arrived and the Community Centre was filled to bursting point – Film Theatre supporters on one side, Jan and her defenders on the other, complete with 948 signature petition – and the councillors sandwiched around tables in -between. And so the debate began - various statements in favour and some that were clearly against. Questions were raised, to which I offered a reply and then came a number of comments from councillors that left me utterly disappointed and seriously hacked off – one from Trevor Hawkins who declared that having studied my proposal, he had concluded that *"This makes no business sense"* one from John Geater who claimed *"These figures are guesses"* and another from Frank Huxley who summarised that my proposal was *"Pie in the sky."*

I sat, I listened and I was genuinely saddened that some of my employers had considered it wiser to dismiss my plans to improve the many aspects of their operation, rather than, like those who preferred to back me, take my previous 16 year track record into account, whereby I had never, ever done anything that I felt was anything other than in the best interests of the venue. I have never forgotten those inconsiderate words and never will, but I do get enormous pleasure from knowing that I have proved those doubters entirely wrong.

This was big news locally and even made the front page of the Heritage Coast Gazette, with the headline 'BERTIE GETS CROPPED!' where it was reported that at the crucial vote my proposal had been successful, with seven in favour, two against and two that sat on the fence. In coming to their decision, it was agreed that Jan would be provided with six months notice and would receive a sum of compensation to help her set up her new business, Bertie's II, which is located a little further down the High Street – a much smarter premises and Jan tells me that the outcome was *"the best thing that ever happened to me"*.

It had been an eventful time at the Film Theatre – in more ways than one and it was shortly before the Bertie's saga that my assistant manager Vivian decided to swiftly leave our employment. With his sudden departure, it was necessary to advertise for another assistant and we were inundated with applicants, from which a handful of hopefuls were interviewed by a panel of councillors, the Town Clerk and myself. First through the door was 21 year old Hannah Everett, who was no stranger to the Film Theatre as she had worked at the cinema since she was a spotty teenager and I can honestly say that I never, ever had a problem with her – she was an exceptional member of my team and I was sorry to lose her to university in 2005, although she did return to work at the Film Theatre during the holidays.

Her interview went well – very well, making her a tough candidate to follow and it was evident that, as the process continued, we all preferred Hannah to be assistant number three. I phoned to break the good news to her – the call went like this; *"Hannah, its Wayne. Thanks for coming in today. We were very impressed with your presentation and I'd like to offer you the position of assistant manager."* *"No way! Really?"* was her excited reply. I will never forget that call – it was a nice call to make.

Hannah walked into the cinema office on the 23rd October 2008 and it wasn't long before an initially quiet Hannah soon found her voice – especially when she was reluctantly hauled on stage during one of my children's shows! She quickly proved herself to be a major asset to our operation, with a genuine appreciation for Leiston Film Theatre and a shared desire to see the venue develop, which was just as well, as that team work was about to be demonstrated as we rolled up our sleeves to transform the cinema foyer.

In the coming weeks, a schedule of works was devised that would see us breaking through the wall the day after Bertie's departure, providing a four week period to transform the space from an empty shop into a fully functional foyer. Firstly, local builder Gordon Read arrived to open up the wall dividing the shop and existing foyer. Then, in the following weeks, between the three of us – Stephen, Hannah and myself, we did almost all the work, from the painting and wallpapering, to constructing the counter and partition wall – everything built to accommodate all the equipment and fittings, working many long hours – it wasn't unusual to find Stephen and I working away until the early hours of the morning. Most of Bertie's counters, light fittings and even the electrical sockets were reused. The new foyer steps were built by a local carpenter Michael Adams – a member of the Support Club, the new carpeting was donated by Leiston Carpets, the electrics were installed by local electrician Keith Skilton – another Support Club member and the access ramp was constructed by Fred Carter – a well known local tradesman and paid for by a donation from British Energy at Sizewell B. As promised, the project itself hadn't cost the Leiston tax payer a single penny and there was even a moment when an inquisitive Jan appeared at the door one day, as we were installing the new counter. All fell silent and then she congratulated us on how good it all looked and to celebrate, I paid the much nicer Bertie's II a visit for a haircut a few weeks later!

It was a very proud day when, on the afternoon of Sunday 19th April 2009 and with paint still drying in places, a gathering of invited guests and councillors arrived to enjoy a glass of vino, a sandwich and a nose around the new Peter Free foyer and a celebratory screening of *The Boat That Rocked.* I think the wine helped to relieve the bitter taste that some councillors still had concerning the project and the grand opening even made the front page of the Heritage Coast Gazette again, with the headline 'FILM THEATRE FOYER SUCCESS' with the editor summarising that despite being controversial, *"There have been no losers here."*

We still have the odd one or two call into our foyer, looking for a haircut. We always explain that Bertie's has moved to more luxurious premises and point them in the right direction.

With the dust now well and truly settled, the foyer finally having a bright and cheerful presence on the High Street and customers stating that, at last the Film Theatre was looking like a 'proper' cinema, the council abandoned their 2008 decision to replace the existing wooden fascia for an identical design, in favour of – cue the fanfare – aluminium signage in 'Palladium Red' with bespoke gold lettering of LEISTON FILM THEATRE – cue the applause! It was now generally considered that the only remaining authentic feature on the front exterior was the black and white beams above the signage and there is no way I'd ever want to see this feature altered or removed. The benefit of the new aluminium version was that it would be almost maintenance free and with the added commitment to complete the project with a fresh coat of paint to the upper woodwork and the introduction of up-lighting to showcase the building in all its after dark glory, it felt that almost everyone was finally singing from the same 'How to transform a cinema' song sheet!

Let me share a private thought with you. There have been a few odd occasions when I have felt somewhat sorry for the members of the Town Council! They bought this cinema in 1976, with nobody really knowing how the business worked and in the early years of their ownership, they did their very best to improve the facility, under the *"that'll do"* eye of dear old Peter Free. They continued to pump money into the town's cinema throughout the 1980's, they leased it in the 1990's and then somebody decided it would be a good idea to advertise for an assistant manager – *"someone with initiative"* and then I arrived and consequently spent the next 21 years going from one initiative to another.

I make this comment because to be quite honest, once we had updated the sound system in 2008, enlarged the foyer in 2009 and introduced new signage in 2010 and were actually making financial progress, I thought we had actually accomplished all that we set out to achieve and I was starting to think that it may be time for me to move on.

Then, during one of our visits to London to meet with the various film distributors, Hannah and I noted that there was much talk of the need to go digital – not from one distributor, but from the majority of them. The fact was that the film companies were slowly reducing the quantity of 35mm film prints that they produced, in favour of the digital drives and that eventually, cinemas that didn't embrace digital cinema and make the necessary investment would have to wait longer to get their hands on a copy of a 35mm film, or even worse, where no 35mm prints had been produced, they wouldn't be able to screen certain films – not an immediate prospect, but certainly one that would definitely occur within a few years. I was, as was many cinema exhibitor, filled with great concern at this situation and my immediate thought was that, on raising this issue with the powers that be in Leiston, the councillors would be forgiven if they were to quietly mutter the words *"what does he want now?"* when the time actually came.

We returned from London genuinely bothered by all this and immediately started doing our homework – what projector would be best and if we were to invest in going digital, should we go 3D as well and if so, which system was most suitable for Leiston? We attended an industry seminar in London, which was packed with anxious cinema owners, who were addressed by those in the know, who confirmed what we had already be told – that digital cinema was expanding at an incredible rate – faster than anyone had imagined. On return to the Film Theatre, I explained the scenario in detail with the Town Clerk and pretty soon, a meeting of the council's Film Theatre committee was arranged so that Hannah and I could brief councillors on the situation. They received a thorough presentation that ultimately recommended that the venue ought to invest in digital projection – not just a digital projector, but (gulp) full automation, a new screen and 3D to boot. There were lots of customers who were travelling to Cineworld in Ipswich to see 3D films and if Leiston could become a 3D screen, we could boast to be the only 3D cinema between Ipswich and Norwich. We'd been at the back of the technological queue for far too long and I saw this as an opportunity for us to jump to the front.

The total cost was going to be in the region of a whopping £75,000 and the Town Council simply couldn't lay their hands on that kind of money willy-nilly. An organisation known as the Digital Funding Partnership had been formed by the Cinema Exhibitors Association – the body that represents the exhibition sector in the UK and were dedicated in assisting independent cinemas to go digital by helping to fund the installation of the necessary projection equipment, through a central loan system and this financial assistance came with a 50 page contract, which worried me, so much so that I arranged an informal meeting in London and intended to ask one simple question – *"If you were us and were able to go digital independently, rather than opt into the DFP scheme, what would you do?"* The answer was an honest *"We would remain independent."*

There was an option of funding available to the Town Council, in the form of a government based, low interest loan and if the council were to prefer this option, they would be required to fund the loan repayments for five years. Thankfully, with a little bit of forward thinking, the council had initiated a projector replacement fund several years earlier, to help fund any major repairs or replacement of their 35mm projector. Due to them buying wisely back in 1988, there had been no significant reason for them to draw on these funds and consequently, there was £25,000 in reserve to put towards their digital purchase. However, this would still leave them £50,000 short.

The Film Theatre Support Club had been 'simmering' away for a couple of years since their substantial financial contribution to improve the stage facilities. With a programme of fund raising activities, the club were now in a position to provide a donation of £11,000 towards this project, leaving a balance of £39,000 to source. Then, in a bold move, the Support Club actually offered to service the repayments on the loan, should the council wish to proceed. I cannot express how grateful I was to the Support Club committee for such an amazing statement. Knowing how many other smaller venues around the country were struggling to comprehend their funding of the digital conversion, I couldn't help but feel so very, very proud of this unprecedented move from the Support Club committee.

Only an absolute fool would have turned their back on such a generous offer and after discussion, the Town Council accepted the loan and the equipment was promptly ordered from Omnex Pro Film, who had installed the digital sound system at the Film Theatre in 2008 and once again provided an unrivalled service during our selection of digital equipment.

Now please pay attention – Leiston Film Theatre Support Club have supported every single loan repayment on the digital equipment since 2010 and at the time of completing this book, are hoping to have enough funds to fully settle this loan ahead of its repayment completion date. There are some people who continually fail to recognise this fact and prefer to imagine that the loan is yet another financial burden on the town. This is simply not the case.

The digital installation required us to close the venue for five days and when the big day finally arrived – a day that had been delayed, by nine weeks, due to a shortage of projector parts (such was the worldwide demand), I was both excited and hesitant. This was an expensive and heavy piece of kit that we would be manoeuvring. I also felt somewhat saddened to think that we wouldn't screen any 35mm film anymore – actual film had played such a huge part of my life and I had a genuine affection for the stuff and I knew how to take care of the film if it went wrong – I didn't know where to start with digital – I struggled to operate the Sky+ box!

Tony from Omnex arrived with his bags of gadgets and gizmos. Tony was (and still is) a proper smart-arse and a complete know-it-all – and for one very good reason – simply because he is so well acquainted when it comes all things technical – and just as well, as we didn't have the first clue where to start! The projector shell arrived in two large parts, with countless boxes containing everything else that was required to make it all work. With a posse of volunteers, each half of the projector was carefully lifted up to a first floor emergency fire door, which was the only access route available other than removing a section of the roof. To our relief (although this had already been assessed earlier) there was a centimetre of space either side to manoeuvre the projector through the narrow doorway and into the projection room – snug would be an understatement and boy, was it heavy. Thankfully, the enlargement of the projection room in 1998 and that fact that the room had two portholes meant that we were able to retain our 35mm projector, just in case the digital went down and we had to revert back to proper film. On a couple of rare occasions it has and we did!

With the projector finally in place, Tony set to work on installing the umpteen components and cables and a very good job he did of it too – as you would expect from a professional clever-clogs! In a nutshell, a digital projection system is a highly complex batch of multiple computers and components that all communicate with each other to send an image through to the projector end of the equipment, where another host of wires and units deliver a superior, high resolution image on the screen (thanks Tony – I told you he was a smart arse!)

After a couple of days cooped up in the projection room, Tony advised us that if we took our seats, we could enjoy a sample of movie trailers in digital quality and some in 3D. Hannah and I took our seats – with a tub of popcorn of course and we spent the next 20-or-so minutes watching clip after clip in pristine digital quality – and I was impressed, seriously impressed. I'd experienced digital cinema in one of those large and impersonal multiplex auditoriums, but it never looked as good as it seemed to on our brand new screen – yes, we invested in a brand new screen too! The picture quality was outstanding – the sound was incredible – the 3D was amazing! Suddenly, my concern of losing 35mm film had vanished and I was filled with great excitement at what we now had – Suffolk's oldest cinema now had the very latest technology. We had come a very, very long way. Digital and 3D projection finally arrived at Leiston Film Theatre on Friday 24th September 2010, to a resounding thumbs-up from our customers.

With the inclusion of full automation, we even had a projector that was capable of starting itself, dimming the lights, opening the curtains, altering the masking, changing the sound levels – in fact, providing that we'd programmed it correctly, the projector could run the show, without us even having to enter the projection room, apart from switching it on and turning it off! We also didn't have to carry those heavy film cans up that spiral staircase anymore – no joke when you're showing 11 reels of *Lord of the Rings*. The films now arrived on a digital drive, similar in appearance to an old 8-track cartridge, that are inserted into the digital server that 'ingests' the film on to the system.

We decided that the projector needed a name, so that we had something to refer to in front of the customer if things went wrong. We named it Peter and in the coming weeks, as we experienced minor teething problems of going digital, comments such as *"Peter's behaving himself this week"* and *"Peter's not very happy"* could be heard around the foyer. It took staff a while to cotton on exactly what we were referring to, but now all staff acknowledge that Peter can sometimes be temperamental and usually when we are really busy – like the time we were showing the multi Oscar winning *The Kings Speech*. It was a wet Wednesday afternoon and the auditorium was packed in a sea of silver hair and five minutes from the end of the film, the office phone rang. *"The sound is cutting in and out"* – I went to investigate and from the projection room I could see that the film had reached its climatic ending where Colin Firth struggles with his stammer, to deliver 'that speech'. Quite ironically, at the very part where King George VI should overcome his stammer, the sound was cutting in and out – a little like comedian Norman Collier used to do with his faulty microphone routine.

I immediately telephoned Tony and explained the situation – and his advice? *"Turn it off, leave it five minutes, and then turn it on again."* Now this may sound simple, but this is actually a 10-15 minute exercise while you wait for the various bits and pieces to wake up. I did as I was told and verbally advised the audience accordingly.

Five minutes later, I powered up the projector and 10 minutes later, using one of the advantages of digital, I was able to jump straight to that particular part of the film. The phone rang again – *"It's still jumping."* I telephoned Tony once more and explained that Colin Firth was still struggling with the script! *"Turn it off again, leave it five minutes, then try again."* I returned to the poor patrons, who had now been sitting there for well over 20 minutes and explained my situation, stating that I would try one more time if they were willing to be patient – and they were.

Okay. Third time lucky. I switched the projector on and with everything crossed, I clicked the play button. The phone rang yet again – *"It's even worse now."* I stopped the film, went into the auditorium now filled with mumbles, broke the bad news that I was unable to show the remainder of the film and apologised (not that it was my fault – it was bloody Peter!) Everyone was offered a complimentary ticket to enjoy the film on another evening, or even a refund if they preferred. A voice cried out from the centre aisle – *"Have we missed much? What happens?"* I explained that Firth gives the speech, walks out onto the balcony, waves to the crowds and that's it. *"Well that's good enough for me!"* came the reply and with that, an understanding audience politely left the Film Theatre and not one of them asked for their money back.

We had to cancel the evening screening and on Tony's arrival the following morning to rectify the problem, the film played perfectly – typical. There have been the odd occasions when Peter has been less than compliant with our instructions, though thankfully these times are few and far between. I can remember Neville Parry saying to me many years ago that you can have hundreds of great shows and nobody says anything about it, but you have one where it goes wrong and everyone knows about it – how very true.

There is a wonderful documentary entitled *The Last Projectionist,* which celebrates the renaissance of independent cinema and details the digital predicament faced by cinemas in the UK in 2012. The film features a group of aging projectionists, all reminiscing around a pub table about their experiences in the projection room and their thoughts on the arrival of digital cinema. The film also tells of the films' director and cinema owner, Tom Lawes, who purchased and refurbished the former Electric Cinema in Birmingham, transforming it from a derelict shell into a going concern. We were lucky enough to present the Suffolk premier of this film in 2012, with the director present – it's a terrific film and I would urge anyone who has a passion for these little gems of cinema to see this film. As a shameless plug, if you purchased this book early enough, you'll be able to enjoy a special screening of *The Last Projectionist* as part of our centenary celebrations on Sunday 23rd March 2014, with all seats priced at 100 pennies for 100 years (it took us ages to think that one up!). The film will be followed by an informal question and answer session with my old 'Chief' Neville Parry – I'm really looking forward to welcoming Nev to the Film Theatre.

Now that this project was completed, there really wasn't anything requiring major investment – much to the relief of the Town Council I'm sure! It was now paramount that, in having such a smart, modern and versatile venue, it was merely a question of maintaining the building – inside and out and that's where Stephen Ginger and I enter. Between us, we spend many hours each year repairing this, painting that and doing whatever else requires attention to keep the old place looking its best and to save money.

The ins and outs of what we do at the Film Theatre are very much our business – the secrets to our success. With the introduction of a projector that was capable of doing everything except sweeping the auditorium floor, this offered us an opportunity to cut expenditure at the Film Theatre by consciously deciding not to replace projection staff as they left our employment. Hannah and I completely tore apart the operation of the venue, scrutinising every outgoing and analysing the income. The cinema was still in tough financial times and now that my 18 year shopping list was complete, drastic decisions had to be made to prove that the business was still viable.

There are many people who believe that we spend all day watching films and eating popcorn and this couldn't be further from the reality that is a constant effort to keep on top of a considerable workload – perhaps we make it look too easy!

This versatile venue could now boast a comfortable auditorium, new stage lighting, a 'proper' foyer, West End cinema sound, state-of-the-art digital projection and was the only 3D cinema for 25 miles. With our financial agenda all prepared and ready to roll out, Hannah and I were going to do our very, very best to reduce the cinema's deficit, prove the believers right and stick two firm fingers up at those pessimists.

It was May 2011 and I was handed an end of year balance sheet for the Film Theatre. Since the Town Council had saved the cinema in 1976, the place had run at a loss and only ever made a small profit in 1994. Some claimed that the cinema was a financial burden on the town – others declared that it was worth every penny. You see, it's very easy to cast criticism, but what must be considered is the fact that in purchasing the cinema – for the town, there was a tremendous amount of work that had to be done to maintain and improve the neglected Picture House – much of which was instigated far too late, hence the enormous spend on the Film Theatre from 1994. Without such investment, the audiences would have stayed away but in committing to see the venture through, the venue underwent the most extensive of refurbishment programmes and in return the audiences steadily returned.

Anyway, with my soapbox tucked away, let's get back to the story. The deficit of the venue had peaked in 2007/2008 at £48,000 and in 2009/2010, the venue had lost almost £33,000. Now, 12 months later, I studied the sheet – income, then expenditure – and again – and one more time. My mouth fell open – we'd made a profit. In 12 months, we'd gone from a major deficit to a small profit. I looked at the sheet one more time to make sure. The enlargement of the foyer, our complete restructuring of the business operation and the installation of the digital projection and 3D equipment had all contributed to this financial success.

We had one of our pantomime script-writing sessions that same day and when we had finished, I asked Stephen and Hannah to stay behind as I had something to tell them. I think they thought I was going to say that I was leaving, but instead I pulled out a bottle of expensive plonk, which had been in storage since my 40th birthday a few months earlier and with a huge grin on my face, I broke the good news to them. As my closest colleagues, I wanted to share this with them and we sat sipping champagne in disbelief for a while. The same thing happened in 2010/2011 and again in 2011/2012 – well, £300 loss to be precise, but only due to my ordering new fire doors! Nevertheless, we were obviously doing something right – and we knew exactly what we were doing.

We have never, nor can we ever take this current success for granted. Each year brings new challenges and we are only ever as busy as the films that are released. Every April, we begin a 12 month struggle to keep the Film Theatre going and to make ends meet. It's never easy and we are fortunate to have such loyal customers and generous supporters – without them, we'd probably have been closed years ago.

The Bright Sparks pantomime in 2012 (Jack and the Beanstalk) proved to be highly problematic backstage, with a severe lack of space resulting in many of the cast having to seek refuge in the cramped garage – hardly the most desirable of dressing rooms in a cold January. The 40 strong cast had been quietly suffering with this for a few years now and with it being inappropriate to house young boys and girls with adult men and woman, this had brought the issue to a head and the general opinion was that something had to be done about it, or risk losing the annual pantomime.

And so, in July 2012, just when councillors were breathing a heavy sigh of relief, I beckoned another meeting of the council's Film Theatre committee and toured them all round the venue, detailing first hand, the scenario that was faced – and not just during the pantomime. A local dance school refused to use the venue because of the lack of backstage facilities and we were unable to produce numerous other shows, due to the cramped conditions behind the scenes.

My preferred option was an open plan first floor extension on top of the existing space, which could be utilised as a multi-use studio –

exhibitions, classes, meetings, functions and, of course, vital additional dressing room facilities. This space could have great potential to further diversify the use of the venue, but would be very, very expensive – early indications suggested that it may cost in the region of £200,000 and this sat uncomfortably with some councillors, who despite my proven acumen, still doubted my initiative and preferred to see any extension built on the derelict grounds at the rear of the building, rather than expanding upwards. Thankfully, a surveyor's report confirmed that this opinion would have proved more costly and certainly wouldn't provide the earning potential that a swanky studio would – and that's very important, because when it comes to funding this project, the council would probably have to rely on a further government loan and these repayments would stand more chance of being balanced by a desirable space, rather than a block build with no appeal whatsoever.

There were (and still are) various funding options available to assist in finding the necessary cash to bring this build to fruition. One of these considerations is to sell a slice of the land at the rear of the Film Theatre. This land has always been referred to as 'derelict ground' – it is commonly used by many local residents to let their dogs foul on and is of no useful purpose whatsoever, other than a car park for staff and visiting artistes. In fact, since day one, this strip of land has been brought up in discussion more times than I care to remember – for sale and to let. Personally, I see this as an ideal opportunity to tidy up this area of waste-ground, whilst reducing the loan amount required to fund the project.

With the help of architect Craig Driver, we devised a plan for a contemporary, multi-use facility – the best that can be achieved in the space that is available, although this wasn't welcomed by the neighbouring properties, who had counter charged that the proposed build would blight their sunlight. Once our plans had been adjusted to allow the sun to continue shining on the residents of Drovers Yard, the scheme was unanimously accepted by the powers that be at Suffolk Coastal's planning department.

151

A collection of meetings were arranged and at the start of one particular 'crunch' meeting, I was unexpectedly presented with a crystal award for 21 years service to Leiston Film Theatre, prior to the start of any discussions. I was genuinely thrilled to have received this recognition from my bosses and after thanking those in attendance, responded by displaying a sheet of paper with the word VISION printed on it. This notice was positioned accordingly, so that all those present could refer to it during the various topics of conversation. This was a fairly lengthy, but informal meeting, during which it was clarified that time was ticking away if we were to embark on this proposed project for completion during our forthcoming centenary year in 2014. I left that meeting feeling optimistic that my opinions had been taken into account and that most of those around the table were in agreement.

At the time of writing this, an ardent Town Council have voted almost unanimously to proceed to tender on the project and I have my fingers firmly crossed that, providing that the returning tenders are appropriate, that the necessary funding becomes available and that councillors maintain their current desire to pursue this scheme, the Film Theatre can look forward to the opening of the Frank Walker Studio (well it had to be didn't it?) at some point in 2014 – our 100th anniversary.

The final reel

Each film has a final reel. This final chapter of a movie can leave an audience in suspense, tears, aching with laughter and on some occasions, wondering what on earth they've been watching for the past two hours! Usually, the last spool takes the opportunity to clear up a few loose ends – to make sense of what has come before – to reveal the big plot twist or a heroic finale. Well, the final words of this book are simply a few miscellaneous ramblings – my opportunity to offer some final thoughts.

I remain utterly amazed and proud that Leiston should be the home of one of the country's oldest surviving cinemas. Where so many larger towns and indeed cities lost their picture palace years ago, this small, rural town retains its very own cinema – and it does indeed belong to the town – the local tax payer is currently paying just 18p per week to have a cinema on their doorstep – although technically it hasn't cost the town anything for the past three years. There are still some who begrudge that 18p per week, ignorant of the huge significance that the Film Theatre has to Leiston – not only is it of historical importance to the area, it also attracts thousands of visitors to the town each year to enjoy the latest films and superb stage shows, putting goodness knows how much additional revenue into the local economy.

The Town Council literally saved Leiston Picture House in 1976 and as demonstrated in the preceding pages, did what they thought was best to keep the place going and hats off to them for doing just that – other local authorities had turned their backs on rescuing their local cinema years earlier. However, it was only really in 1992 that things really started to happen at Leiston Film Theatre. New councillors, a new Town Clerk, the formation of the Film Theatre Support Club and a new assistant manager – all working together, with an overwhelming perseverance to not only see the cinema remain, but to exploit its true potential and although it took a number of years to carefully advance, we have eventually seen our ambitions prevail.

A Town Council is comprised of members of that community – shop keepers, nurses and the like – all with an opinion and every good intention, but none with the expertise in operating a cinema – and neither did I in 1992, having defected from the projection room into management, but I quickly learnt, mainly through experience and I would like to believe that my track record has demonstrated that I genuinely care for this wonderful venue and, 21 years later, know exactly what I am doing. I am not one to sit on my backside, waiting for my pay slip each month – if I was, the cinema wouldn't be what it is now. If the venue is to continue as it is today and to improve further, the owners must trust the advice of their management. Vision is a wonderful attribute to possess.

I can't believe that I have actually completed this book. It's taken me a couple of years to write this, on and off, and has at times been a complete chore, but at the same time in researching the incredible history of the old place, I have been instilled with a renewed respect in being part of its unique history. This book has three main objectives – to capture the, as yet, untold story of Suffolk's oldest cinema, to celebrate the fact that Leiston is the home of a 100 year old cinema and to educate the people of Suffolk and far beyond that the Film Theatre exists and is no longer the 'flea-pit' it once was – we now have a brilliant venue to be immensely proud of.

There have been times when I've been asked *"Have you ever thought about moving on to a bigger cinema?"* and my answer has always remained the same. I could never work for a multiplex cinema chain – I don't like them. Yes, I visit them every now and again, but I can't stand them. I consider them impersonal, expensive, noisy and with no sense of individuality whatsoever. I believe that an independent cinema – single screen or multi, that is managed by those who care for the venue, offers a superior service, where the customer is far more than just a ticket number. I have remained at the Film Theatre because it has something of a hold over me – it's more than a job – it's like a marriage of sorts and quite a relationship it's been too! We had a blind date in 1992 and despite having serious doubts initially whether this relationship would actually work, a bizarre bond quickly developed between us. There are times when I absolutely adore my job and there are occasions when I simply despair (you can guess when) and would quite happily divorce myself from it! Thankfully, the good times overshadow the bad. The believers overrule the doubters. If I wasn't so fond of the old place, I 'd have been gone years ago.

There has been many times when I've asked Stephen Ginger *"Whatever would Frank Walker say if he could see his Picture House now?"* I think he would approve – he was the one who brought a cinema to Leiston and he quickly learnt how precarious the business was in its infancy. The fact that it is still here and actually holding its own would provoke a nod and a smile I'm sure. And as for Peter Free? Well, he lived to see his beloved Picture House undergo a major transformation before he passed away in 2006 and if he could see it now, with its new fascia and equipment, as it approaches its celebratory year, there is only one word that he would mutter ... *"Unbelievable!"*

If I could travel back to any one point in time, it would definitely be the 27th October 1914 – the opening day of Leiston Picture House. To study the historic paperwork and images of the day is one thing, but to have been part of such a magnificent event in its day must have been a wonderful experience. Leiston Picture House cost £3,057 to build in 1914, was sold in 1976 for £12,500 and is now probably worth in the region of £750,000 (as a going concern).

In 2014, Leiston Film Theatre will celebrate its magnificent centenary with an ambitious programme of 100 separate events and promotions to commemorate this remarkable achievement. The year long celebrations will provide an opportunity for all those who genuinely appreciate our wonderful venue, to join us for what we promise will be a memorable 12 months.

I am fortunate to have a terrific team at the Film Theatre and they have my thanks for all that they do. Hannah – you are a wonderful colleague to work alongside and although I fear that, unlike myself, you won't be spending 21 years running this cinema, you have played a significant part in what we have accomplished. Stephen – your encouragement, belief and the hours that you donate, caring for the cinema is admirable and I count myself fortunate to have somebody like you on 'my side'. Unlike Hannah, I *can* see you still pottering around the Film Theatre when you are 70 – now there's a thought!

I think it would be safe to say that I've proven to my father that, despite being a certain annoyance at the time, my commandeering of the garden shed all those years ago, to transform it into a cinema or a puppet theatre wasn't in vain and that despite all the past disagreements, this 'mistake' has made him proud – I know this because he has told me so. Now aged 87, he still pops into the cinema with Jean twice a week to enjoy a quick catch-up and a cuppa, although I do wish he'd get his hearing aid sorted! In recent years, he's helped me raise thousands of pounds for the Film Theatre Support Club, by permitting us to be the only cinema to screen his vast collection of archive photographs of Aldeburgh. Thanks Dad – for everything you've done. Only last week, I showed him the cover for my book, which he studied in great detail before saying that mum would be so very proud if she could see this.

So what of the future for Leiston Film Theatre? Well, hopefully we can look forward to the opening of the Frank Walker Studio in 2014, to enable the venue to further expand and diversify. I'd also like to get my hands on the remaining shop unit, currently occupied by the friendly Chiropodist, but after the hoo-ha over the barbers shop though, I think I'll have to bide my time on that one! The Film Theatre Support Club have played such a vital role in our success (are you a member?), raising in excess of £140,000 in 21 years and they have my heartfelt appreciation for all that they have done and continue to do. I would like to imagine that the Town Council, Support Club and Film Theatre management will continue to work closely together, with a common objective of prolonging the current and future capabilities of the town's cinema. The way I see it, now that Leiston has a comfortable, versatile and technologically advanced venue, every effort must be made to maintain that reputation that we've all strived so hard to achieve. Celebrating a centenary is one thing – and we certainly will, but it is paramount that people remain loyal to their local cinemas to retain their existence – we are very lucky to have three fine independent cinemas within an 18 mile radius, where other small towns have lost theirs. The point I'm making is that you must never take these intimate cinema's for granted. Keep supporting us – we'll keep showing the films and putting on a show, providing that you keep putting your bums on our seats.

And me? I love my work and writing this book has reinforced that emotion. I have known many people who absolutely hate their jobs - statistics advise us that we spend 11 years working during our lifetime! I can honestly say that, even after 21 years at the Film Theatre, it's a rare occasion when I resent turning out for work – and I realise that I am very lucky in this respect. I don't intend to be at the Film Theatre forever and at some point, when I consider my job is finally done, I may step aside and support whoever would be next to carry the venue forward. With the prospect of exciting developments ahead, this won't happen too soon, so the council will have to wonder what 'initiative' I will come up with next!

And so, with the popcorn well and truly spilt, I will end my book by recalling a comment about the Film Theatre that was found quite unexpectedly on the internet – a remark that, after all that we have accomplished since 1992, in transforming Leiston Film Theatre into a venue of envious proportions, really does say it all. The comment read *"It is the best cinema we have been to for years, puts all Showcase and the like to shame."*

And who would I be to argue?